D1546582

FIELD MARSHAL
# Sam Manekshaw
## THE MAN AND HIS TIMES

# FIELD MARSHAL
# Sam Manekshaw
## The Man and His Times

BRIGADIER BEHRAM M. PANTHAKI (RETD)
AND ZENOBIA PANTHAKI

NIYOGI
BOOKS

**Overseas Distribution**

USA and Canada
**ACC Distribution**
email: sales@accdistribution.com
www.accdistribution.com

United Kingdom, Ireland, Europe and Africa
**Kodansha Europe Ltd.**
email: info@kodansha.eu
www.kodansha.eu

Cambodia, Burma, Laos and Thailand
**Paragon Asia Co. Ltd.**
email: info@paragonasia.com
www.paragonasia.com

Published by
**NIYOGI BOOKS**
D-78, Okhla Industrial Area, Phase-I
New Delhi-110 020, INDIA
Tel: 91-11-26816301, 49327000
Fax: 91-11-26810483, 26813830
email: niyogibooks@gmail.com
website: www.niyogibooksindia.com

Text ©: Brigadier Behram M. Panthaki (Retd) and Zenobia Panthaki

Editor: Sucharita Ghosh
Design: PealiDezine

ISBN: 978-93-83098-30-9
Publication: 2014
First reprint: 2015

The responsibility of any kind for the correctness and legality of the facts stated or opinion expressed in the book is entirely of the author and not of the publishers.

All rights are reserved. No part of this publication may be reproduced or transmitted in any form or by any means, electronic or mechanical, including photocopying, recording or by any information storage and retrieval system without prior written permission and consent of the publisher.

Printed at: Niyogi Offset Pvt. Ltd., New Delhi, India.

Dedicated to
men in uniform who laid down their lives defending this country
and to their widows whose sacrifice is in equal measure

# Contents

# Foreword

Brigadier Behram Panthaki, ably assisted by his wife, Zenobia, has written this excellent book on Field Marshal S.H.F.J. Manekshaw, popularly known as Sam, who led the Indian Army to a historic and unprecedented victory in 1971. This book is not a biography; it is primarily a personal account by the author of his close association with the field marshal and his family while serving as his ADC.[1] It admirably portrays, through various anecdotes, the character and personality of a great military leader gifted with tremendous wit and sense of humour.

I had the privilege of working with Sam for over two decades and saw him grow from a promising young lieutenant colonel to a field marshal. He did great credit to each appointment he held during his long, illustrious career. For the first ten years our association was friendly and cordial, but for the next decade it came under a cloud due to circumstances beyond my control. However, I did get an opportunity to serve under Sam again and clear the misunderstandings. Sam was more than generous to me.

In 1960 I was appointed staff officer to Lieutenant General B.M. Kaul who at the time was quarter-master general.[2] Because of his close relations with Prime Minister Jawaharlal Nehru and Defence Minister Krishna Menon, Kaul had become all-powerful in the army. Both Menon and Kaul were hostile to Sam for their own reasons. Menon, because Sam had refused to be disloyal to the then army chief, General Thimayya, with whom Menon had differences. Kaul was envious of Sam who was junior to him but far ahead of him professionally and presented a threat to his aspirations to become the army chief.

As his staff officer, I served Kaul loyally, and he rewarded me by nominating me to attend the coveted Joint Services Staff College in the UK for which only one vacancy was available each year and had to be shared among the three services. The army got its turn for this course once every three years. Normally officers in the rank of colonel or even brigadier were sent on this course whereas I was just a major. Since I had attended the Indian Army's staff course ten years earlier, Kaul suggested I go to the Defence Services Staff College (DSSC) in Wellington (south India) and complete a two-week attachment with the naval and air force wings before proceeding to the UK.

---

1 The ADC or Aide-de-Camp (French for camp assistant) is a personal assistant to a general officer.
2 A quarter-master general is in charge of supplies and transport for the army.

*Sam
continued
to rise in
the army ...
In 1969 he
became the
army chief ...*

Sam was a major general and the commandant of the college. Since Kaul and Sam were not on good terms I was seen as 'Kaul's man', sent to spy on the commandant. I arrived at the college to find Sam unlike his usual self, cold towards me and guarded in his speech. While on attachment, late one night I received a message to immediately meet a colonel who had been sent by Kaul from Delhi and was staying at a hotel in Coonoor. When I entered the colonel's room I found two army instructors from the Staff College briefing the colonel and insinuating that Sam had been indulging in 'anti-national' activities. He had paintings of Robert Clive and Warren Hastings[3] retrieved from storage, restored and hung on the walls in his office. They alleged that during a lecture at the Shivaji Hall, in the presence of foreign students, Sam said that the painting of Shivaji[4] riding a stallion was misleading, for Shivaji only rode '*tattoos*' (ponies). The colonel asked me to give similar evidence but I refused since I had not witnessed any anti-national activity by Sam. The colonel was outraged and threatened to call General Kaul. He dialled Delhi several times, but never got through. I walked out of the hotel, relieved but disgusted with the sordid affair. I could not, obviously, apprise Sam of what I had witnessed as I may have been seen as one who carried tales. On my return to Delhi, Kaul sent for me. He was very angry at my refusal to give evidence and threatened to take me off the course in the UK. I was brusquely told to leave his office, which I did with some relief. I received no further communication from him and after three days I sailed for England, as scheduled. While in the UK, I heard that a court of inquiry had been held against Sam and he had been exonerated of all charges levelled against him.

On completing my course I was promoted to lieutenant colonel and posted as instructor at the Defence Services Staff College in Wellington. Sam was still the commandant and continued to be distant with me. Meanwhile Kaul had taken over command of the newly raised 4 Corps along the north-eastern border with China. A few weeks later the 1962 debacle took place when the Chinese walked in and handed us a humiliating defeat. Kaul was removed from command and Sam was promoted to relieve him. This was divine justice.

Sam continued to rise in the army. When he was eastern army commander, I served under him first as a battalion commander in 1965 and then as a brigade commander in 1968. In 1969 he became the army chief and in 1970 I was posted to the newly created Pay Cell in Army Headquarters to submit the army's case to the Third Pay Commission. Indian commissioned officers (ICOs), beginning with the first course which had graduated from the Indian Military Academy in 1934, had suffered a big pay cut in 1947. Sam's monthly salary as a brigadier was one thousand rupees less than the salary of a brigadier from Sandhurst[5] commissioned a year before him. During the first two Pay Commissions the army had been represented by the Defence Ministry, and thereby denied an opportunity to make a strong case for redress. When Sam became chief he convinced

3 Maj. Gen. Robert Clive was a British officer who established military and political supremacy in India. Clive and Warren Hastings, his successor, secured India for the British Crown.

4 Shivaji Bhosale was the founder of the Maratha Empire of central India, which at its peak encompassed most of the Indian subcontinent.

5 The Royal Military Academy is at Sandhurst, UK, from where Indian officers used to earn their commission prior to 1934 and were known as KCIOs (King's Commissioned Indian Officers).

the government to allow the army to present its case directly to the Third Pay Commission. His retirement was fast approaching and a pay hike for the army would be his parting gift to the service. At that time I did not know the great importance he attached to the task assigned to me and felt that my new posting was not a high profile appointment and spelt the end of my professional career. In spite of feeling sorely disappointed I worked hard and produced a 300-page report for the Pay Commission. Sam was very appreciative of the depth and quality of my work and asked me to make presentations to the army commanders and the chiefs of the other two services.

It was 1971, and before the Pay Commission could examine the army's case and give its award, a war with Pakistan appeared imminent. I had been cleared for promotion to major general and I approached Sam for an operational appointment and an active role in the war. Reminding him of the time we had served together in the Military Operations Directorate in 1946, I joked that the GSO1,[6] Lieutenant Colonel Sam Manekshaw, was going to war with the GSO2, Major Yahya Khan,[7] while I, the GSO3, Captain S.K. Sinha, was being left out of the battle! He had a hearty laugh and told me that I would soon be taking over as Deputy Adjutant General,[8] on promotion. I would have the added responsibility of manpower planning apart from handling the Pay Cell. I had no option but to accept his decision. During the war my responsibilities included mobilising manpower to the battlefront and ensuring that the units had no deficiencies. After the war I had to deal with the stupendous task of managing 92,000 Pakistani prisoners of war (POWs). Our policy was to look after these prisoners so well that they would return to Pakistan as ambassadors of durable peace. We organised *mushairas*,[9] film shows, lectures by Islamic clerics and even cricket matches between our officers and the Pakistani prisoner officers. We allowed American journalists to visit the POW camp in Roorkee. A *Los Angeles Times* correspondent wrote that never in history had prisoners of war been better treated. Sam appointed me to lead an Indian delegation at a conference convened in Italy by the International Red Cross and sponsored by the UN to discuss treatment of POWs. My presentation was much appreciated and earned me kudos from both Sam and Defence Minister Jagjivan Ram.

Sam was appointed field marshal on January 3, 1973. I was the officiating adjutant general and managed with much difficulty to get the bureaucrats to agree to sanction a field marshal's baton for him, but major decisions regarding his salary, perquisites and protocol were kept pending. He was to relinquish his appointment[10] as the army chief on January 15, 1973. I arranged that the annual Army Day Parade would be a farewell for him. For the first and only time in the history of the Indian Army, regimental colours were brought on parade and dipped in salute to him. Only

6 General Staff Officer, Grade 1 is a lieutenant colonel, GSO Grade 2 is a major and GSO Grade 3 is a captain.

7 Maj. Yahya Khan opted for Pakistan at Independence and rose to become army chief and chief marshal law administrator and president in March 1969.

8 The Adjutant General's (AG) branch is responsible for recruitment, discipline, vigilance, ceremonials and welfare.

9 An Urdu poetic symposium.

10 A field marshal never retires, therefore he is deemed to 'relinquish office'. He continues to be a serving officer as long as he lives.

*His retirement was fast approaching and a pay hike for the army would be his parting gift to the service*

*I have the
satisfaction
of paying my
tribute to
the greatest
soldier of the
Indian Army*

heads of state and field marshals are entitled to this unique honour. Sam was overwhelmed. Ten days later, I received intimation that I had been awarded the Param Vishisht Seva Medal (PVSM), the highest military award for outstanding peacetime service. Normally officers in the rank of lieutenant general are given this award on the eve of their retirement. I was then a major general with about ten years of residual service. I realised that this was special recognition that I had been given at the instance of Sam. I went to thank him at the MES[11] Inspection Bungalow where he was living temporarily while finishing touches were being given to his new home in Coonoor. That day I decided to come clean and apprised him of how I had declined to give evidence against him in 1961. He smiled and said that I should have told him much earlier. He was glad I had not suffered on his account.

I have related these details of my long relationship with Sam, to shed light on his character especially his understanding and fairness. In doing so, I have the satisfaction of paying my tribute to the greatest soldier of the Indian Army. I strongly recommend this book to the present generation and to posterity. ◆

Lt Gen. S.K. Sinha (Retd)

---

11 Military Engineering Service, that is in charge of accommodation at all military cantonments.

# Preface

It was by sheer quirk of destiny that I was appointed Aide-de-Camp (ADC) to Lt Gen. Sam Manekshaw. While graduating from the Indian Military Academy (IMA), Dehradun, I had opted for the 8th Gorkha Rifles but ten days before the Passing Out Parade,[1] I learnt that I had been assigned to the Corps of Signals. My morale was in my boots. My company commander, Maj. Ratan Singh Yadava (Army Ordnance Corps), seeing my disappointment, circumvented procedures and arranged for me to speak to Lt Gen. Sam Manekshaw, from the 8th Gorkha Rifles, who was western army commander based in Simla (now Shimla). Desperation trumped protocol and throwing caution to the wind, on a 'strength 1' military trunk line, I pleaded my case. Indiscretion being the lesser part of valour, I threatened to resign if I did not get my choice of arm which I was entitled to since I had stood sixth on the merit list.

I learnt much later that my call had interrupted the general at lunch. After hearing me out he returned to the table and told his family about the strange call he had received from a gentleman cadet 'Beroze'[2] Panthaki at the IMA who wanted to join his regiment. Thanks to the poor connectivity 'Beroze' was what he called me ever after. My request was categorised as a tall order and my threat to quit had only amused him. Luckily for me his daughter, Sherry, prevailed on him to do something for the 'poor bloke' who had mustered the courage to speak to an army commander. He did 'something' indeed, for within forty-eight hours I was transformed into the 'lucky bloke'. An amendment signal was received at the IMA and I was reassigned to the 8th Gorkha Rifles.

On February 9, 1964 I earned my commission as a second lieutenant in the Indian Army and was posted to 58 Gorkha Training Centre[3] (GTC) in Dehradun. In three short months I tired of the mundane duties at a training establishment and wrote to the general, seeking a challenging assignment in an active formation. This time round the 'old man'[4] was convinced that I spelt trouble and needed to be 'fixed'. For a second time he did intercede on my behalf, and within ten days I received my posting order to the 2nd Battalion of the 8th Gorkha Rifles (2/8 GR) which was

---

1 Military graduation ceremony.
2 The correct spelling is Behroze, but the General always spelt it as 'Beroze'.
3 Training Centres impart basic training to recruits prior to their induction into their battalions.
4 'Old man' is a term used in the army for a senior officer.

engaged in counter-insurgency operations in Nagaland.[5] I joined the unit in June. My Commanding Officer (CO), the late Lt Col. Shamsher Singh, was from the old school and believed that subalterns were meant to be seen, not heard. I settled into the routine of an infantry battalion and saw combat action; my dreams finally realised. In December Lt Gen. Sam Manekshaw, who had taken over as eastern army commander, visited the battalion while we were on training in the plains of Assam. Officers and JCOs[6] lined up at Jorhat airport to receive the new army commander. Being the junior-most, I was last in the receiving line. When he approached me I saluted and said, '2nd Lt Panthaki, Sir!' 'So, you are the bugger?' 'Yes Sir,' I replied! That was the sum total of our first encounter.

Six months later, in June 1965, I was summoned to the CO's office one afternoon, ordered to pack my bags and take the air force courier[7] to Calcutta (now Kolkata) the following day. The army commander had asked for me as his ADC. I had no choice as a subaltern. I returned to my basha,[8] packed my worldly possessions in one small trunk and a kitbag and collected my movement order. The next morning I boarded the courier to Calcutta. In a starched cotton uniform, Sam Browne[9] and a Gorkha hat, I reported at the army commander's office. I was ushered into the large room with spartan furnishing. I clicked my heels, saluted and stood at attention for what seemed like an eternity. There was no response and the general remained engrossed in his work. On the floor lay sprawled an Alsatian, a Labrador and a Cocker Spaniel who snored in cadence, and like their master ignored my presence. Finally, the general looked up from his papers and sternly asked, 'Will you work for me?' Before I could respond, I was told to get out and get my instructions from his Assistant Military Secretary (AMS). As I turned on my heels and left his office I thought I was in for a rough ride. The AMS, Lt Col. Rustom Khambatta (Artillery), was made of sterner stuff. I was given a detailed briefing on my role and responsibilities, on dos and don'ts and on the general's likes and dislikes, his quirks and idiosyncrasies. With that I was sent packing to my office and given a stack of files to go through. Mid-morning the army commander walked into my room, gave me the once-over and asked me why I had come to work for him dressed like a Christmas tree, referring to the Sam Browne that is worn only on formal occasions! I replied that I was following my CO's orders. He turned and left without a word, leaving me uneasy and diffident.

I served as ADC to Gen. Manekshaw for two years while he was the eastern army commander, leaving him to join my battalion in NEFA[10] in 1967. In August 1969 I returned as his aide when he became army chief, leaving him briefly to join my battalion during the 1971 war with Pakistan. I continued to serve on his staff till he relinquished office on January 15, 1973 after he was promoted to Field Marshal. In sum, I worked for him for a longer period of time than any officer of the Indian Army and I was fortunate to have had the opportunity to serve a military strategist who changed the map of the Indian subcontinent.

*The purpose of this book is to shed light on his character and on his qualities of head and heart*

---

5 An eastern state of India bordering Burma (now Myanmar).
6 Junior Commissioned Officers (equivalent to Warrant Officers).
7 Indian Air Force flight for service personnel.
8 A thatched hut that is temporary accommodation in a field location.
9 Cross belt.
10 North East Frontier Agency, now known as Arunachal Pradesh.

Field Marshal Sam Manekshaw was an iconic leader that a nation produces but once in many generations. A lot has been written about his military prowess. The purpose of this book is to shed light on his character and on his qualities of head and heart. All of what I recount is through memory for when I served with him, I never thought that I would one day attempt to put pen to paper. The recollections are mostly mine; the writing is my wife's. This book is a portrait of a man who rose to the highest rank in the Indian Army without compromising his core values of honesty, integrity and moral and professional courage. We hope this book will inspire young Indians and reaffirm that humility and integrity are not mutually exclusive.

Our sincere thanks to the Manekshaw family for sharing personal photographs, letters and anecdotes, to Lt Gen. S.K. Sinha for his guidance and for writing the Foreword to this book, to Lt Gen. S.K. Singh, ex-Vice Chief of Army Staff and Colonel of 8th Gorkha Rifles for his support, to the Manekshaw Museum at 58 GTC, Shillong, to my battalion, 2/8 GR, to the many senior, retired officers who served under Sam and readily shared their experiences with us, to our publisher, Niyogi Books India, and to family, friends, coursemates and colleagues who encouraged us to write. ◆

Brig. Behram Panthaki (Retd) and
Zenobia Panthaki

*Sam Manekshaw was an iconic leader that a nation produces but once in many generations*

Sam, the eligible bachelor

FACING PAGE:
The Manekshaw home on
the Mall, Amritsar
Courtesy: The Manekshaw family

# Amritsar
# to
# Dehradun

Sam was born to a Parsi family in Amritsar on April 3, 1914; he was the fifth of six children. The Parsis are a minuscule community that migrated from Persia to India around the eighth century to avoid religious persecution and to preserve their Zoroastrian faith. In India the largest concentration of Parsis is in the city of Bombay (now Mumbai), but almost every family can trace its roots to the state of Gujarat where the community first landed as refugees, and which was home to them for many centuries. With the arrival of the British the Parsis moved to Bombay and evolved into an educated, westernised community. With discipline and honesty, they were quick to make their mark during the days of the British Raj as able administrators. A western education and a liberal outlook saw their advancement in the arts and sciences and in business. Generous and charitable to a fault, over the years they have contributed in large measure to the development of India in every field.

Sam's paternal grandfather, Framji, was a teacher in Valsad, a small town in Gujarat. One of his students was Morarji Desai, a freedom fighter, a Gandhian and India's prime minister from 1977–1979. Sam's father, Hormusji, was born and raised in Valsad but went on to study medicine

at Grant Medical College, Bombay. While still a student, he met and fell in love with the vivacious Hilla Mehta. A long courtship ensued, for the young Hormusji dared not propose till his finances allowed him to take the plunge. He squirrelled away his allowance and as soon as he graduated, he dashed off with his savings to buy a diamond ring from K. Wadia, a famous Bombay jeweller. With some trepidation he proposed to Hilla who readily accepted. They were married in 1899.

Life was not easy. Hormusji's medical practice did not prosper and the couple strived to make ends meet, especially after the birth of their first child, Fali. Seeing the young doctor struggle, friends suggested he move to Lahore where there was a shortage of medical practitioners. The young couple took the plunge and in 1903, with their firstborn and Rs 150 on person, they boarded the Frontier Mail at Bombay Central Railway Station. They settled down in the 'Intermediate Class' compartment reserved for Parsis and Anglo-Indians and after two days they arrived in Amritsar. According to Sam, when his father opened the window shutters, his mother, who was all of eighteen years and had lived all her life in Bombay, panicked at the sight of tall, well-

Sam's parents: Hillabai and Captain Hormusji Manekshaw
Courtesy: The Manekshaw family

built Sikhs[1] with long flowing hair and bushy beards striding the platform. The doctor alighted with his distressed wife and decided to return to Bombay, but once they entered the city they were drawn to it and decided to make Amritsar their home.

Hormusji set up a clinic and pharmacy at Katra Ahluwalia in the heart of the city. He was the only doctor in the vicinity and his practice flourished as did his pharmacy because his prescriptions were formulated and his medicines affordable. Within a short time the couple purchased a 5000-square-yard plot on the Mall, built a home and laid down their roots. The stork made five visits to the Mall Road home. All six children grew up in the Punjab heartland and spoke fluent Punjabi apart from Hindi, English and their mother tongue, Gujarati.

During World War I, Hormusji signed up for Indian Medical Service, a military outfit that also enrolled civilian doctors. He served in Mesopotamia (now Iraq) and later in Egypt, in the rank of captain. When the war was over, he returned to Amritsar and to his practice and began taking an active interest in social welfare activities in the city. He was the founder member of the Rotary Club of Amritsar that was established in 1933. Hilla adjusted well to life in Amritsar. She was friendly with everyone in the mohalla (neighbourhood) and ever ready to give a listening ear or lend a helping hand. The Manekshaws had an active social life and were members of the Services and the Amritsar Club.

At the time, Amritsar had no English medium schools, so Fali, their firstborn, was sent to his maternal grandparents in Bombay. The younger sons, Jan, Sam and Jemi, were boarders at Sherwood College, Nainital, while

---

1 Sikhs are the followers of Sikhism, a religion propagated by Guru Nanak in the fifteenth century.

Sam and his sister, Sheroo
Courtesy: The Manekshaw family

the girls, Cilla and Sheroo, attended the Convent of Jesus and Mary at Murree.[2] As a result, Hilla and Hormusji's home was an empty nest for the greater part of the year. From December to February the children would be at home for their winter vacation and the house would come alive with their pranks and laughter. Hilla was an excellent cook and every meal was a feast of Parsi delicacies.

Of all his siblings, Sam was the most mischievous. He would accompany his father to the Services Club but the many promises to behave would soon be broken and the young boy would invariably get up to one prank or other. It was only the timely intervention of the captain's card

---

2 A hill station near Rawalpindi, now in Pakistan.

*Of all his siblings, Sam was the most mischievous*

*One morning, at the tender age of four ... Sam stomped out of the house after a disagreement with his mother*

partners that saved him from a sound thrashing. One morning, at the tender age of four, while his father was in Egypt, Sam stomped out of the house after a disagreement with his mother. An old Parsi gentleman, out for his morning constitutional, saw the little boy on the street by himself and asked him where he was going. Sam replied confidently that he was going to the police station to lodge a complaint against his mother who was refusing to give him his share of the family fortune even when he told her that he intended to leave home for good. It took considerable coaxing and cajoling by the old gentleman to escort him home and make him patch up with his mother. In retaliation for all the scolding he received, Sam would tell the servants that Hilla was his stepmother, '*Meri maa to angrez hai!*' (My mother is an English lady!) At Sherwood College the same boisterous nature got him into many scraps.

Sam was a terrible tease and his victims were often his siblings. One time he sent his younger brother Jemi literally flying in the air after he cajoled him to firmly plant two of his fingers in an electrical outlet. Another time, when his parents were taking their afternoon nap, he raised Jemi on his shoulders and told him to retrieve a tin of biscuits from the top shelf of a cupboard. Jemi reached out with both hands and clung to the shelf bringing it down with all its contents with a loud crash that disturbed his parents' siesta. Sam was in the dock again.

The most frequent target of Sam's rowdiness was his sister, Sheroo. They would argue till they came to fisticuffs at which point Cilla and Jan would intervene and pull them apart. When Sam was restrained he would try and spit at his sister from a distance. In retaliation Sheroo would tell everyone, including the servants, that when she grew up, she would marry and have a house of her own and when her brothers came visiting, she would serve Fali, Jan and Jemi chicken and duck but for Sam she would cook only *dodhi* (white pumpkin)! As is often the case, when they grew up Sam was very fond of Sheroo as she of him. Each time he visited her home in Bombay she would lay out a lavish spread, while Sam never failed to ask, 'Sheroo, I'm still waiting for the *dodhi.*'

**FROM LEFT TO RIGHT:**
**Sam, Cilla, Jan and Sheroo**
Courtesy: The Manekshaw family

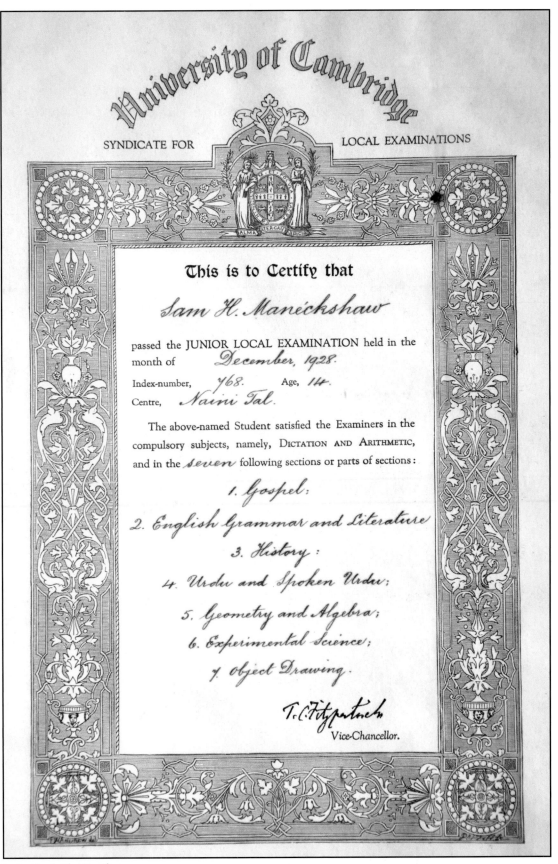

**University of Cambridge**

SYNDICATE FOR

LOCAL EXAMINATIONS

This is to Certify that

*Sam H. Manéckshaw*

passed the JUNIOR LOCAL EXAMINATION held in the month of *December, 1928.*

Index-number, *768.* Age, *14.*

Centre, *Naini Tal.*

The above-named Student satisfied the Examiners in the compulsory subjects, namely, DICTATION AND ARITHMETIC, and in the *seven* following sections or parts of sections:

1. *Gospel:*

2. *English Grammar and Literature*

3. *History:*

4. *Urdu and Spoken Urdu;*

5. *Geometry and Algebra;*

6. *Experimental Science;*

7. *Object Drawing.*

*T. C. Fitzpatrick*
Vice-Chancellor.

**Junior Cambridge Certificate**
Courtesy: The Manekshaw family

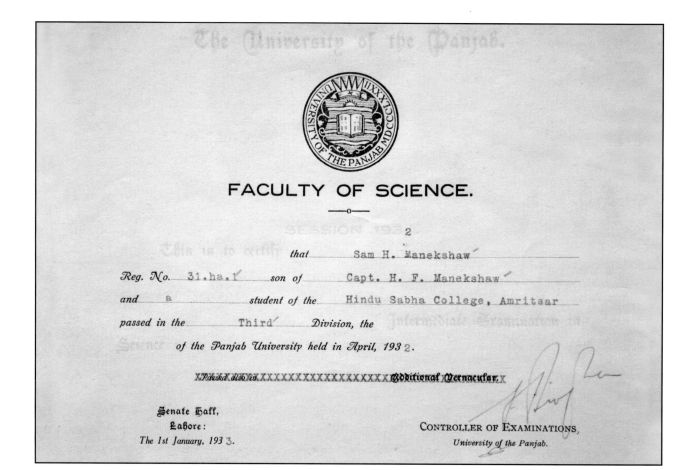

## FACULTY OF SCIENCE.
——o——

This is to certify that    Sam H. Manekshaw

Reg. No.  31.ha.1   son of    Capt. H. F. Manekshaw

and    a    student of the    Hindu Sabha College, Amritsar

passed in the    Third    Division, the

of the Panjab University held in April, 1932.

X Passed also in XXXXXXXXXXXXXXXXXXXX Additional Vernacular. X

Senate Hall,
Lahore:
The 1st January, 1933.

CONTROLLER OF EXAMINATIONS,
University of the Panjab.

**Certificate from the University of the Panjab**
Courtesy: The Manekshaw family

All the Manekshaw children were successful professionals. Fali qualified as an engineer from the UK and worked for Stewarts and Lloyds in Calcutta. Cilla, the elder daughter, taught English at Khalsa College, Amritsar. Jan, the second son earned an engineering degree from the UK and worked for British Insulated Callender's Cables (which later became Indian Cables) in Calcutta. He retired as the director of the company. Sheroo was a qualified teacher from St Bede's College, Simla. Sam was the fifth child. At birth his parents had named him Cyrus after the mighty Persian warrior king, but an aunt who heard of this was very upset for at the time a Parsi gentleman by name of Cyrus had earned a great deal of notoriety and had been marched off to jail. What's in a name? Well, obviously quite a lot for the aunt prevailed and his name was changed to Sam. The youngest was Jemi who like his father became a doctor, earning his degree from the Medical College in Lahore. He joined the Indian Air Force and retired in the rank of air vice marshal. The Manekshaw siblings were close-knit and remained so throughout their lives. Sam was the indulgent, ever-obliging brother and uncle, adored by his nieces and nephews. Of course he was a very special grandfather to his three grandchildren.

As a child Sam was extremely fond of his father and would accompany him on visits to patients and to his pharmacies. His boyhood ambition was to study medicine. Knowing that his son could not stay away from mischief Hormusji dangled before him the bait of sending him to

England for higher studies if he did well in high school. This motivated Sam. He stopped playing games and toiled at his books, otherwise not his strongest suit, and passed his Senior Cambridge[3] examination in 1931 with distinction.

Sam had held up his end of the bargain, but his father had second thoughts. Hormusji had reservations about leaving a seventeen-year-old rumbustious boy unsupervised. Besides, he had financial constraints with two sons already studying in the UK, so he suggested Sam wait out the year and had him admitted to the Hindu Sabha College in Amritsar. Heartbroken and resentful, Sam did not speak much to his father for eighteen months; behaviour that he regretted in later years.

In 1932 the British established the Indian Military Academy (IMA) at Dehradun for young men aspiring to join the army as commissioned officers. Sam borrowed money from his mother, went to Delhi, and took the entrance examination for the IMA. He stood sixth in the order of merit and, on October 1, 1932, he was admitted as a Gentleman Cadet (GC).

For the first ten weeks along with his coursemates, Sam spent most of his time on the drill square under the watchful gaze of a sergeant major who bellowed orders and drilled the young men for hours until they perfected their routine. The academy combined strenuous physical and small arms training with lectures on junior-level leadership and military tactics. The young men who entered its portals were transformed into officers and gentlemen; disciplined, courteous, well-mannered and immaculately turned out. Because of his good academic scores in English and mathematics Sam was initially assigned to 'B' Company, Woolwich Wing, that trained officers for technical arms like Engineering and Signals.[4] But his grades slipped and Sam was transferred to Sandhurst Wing where officers were trained for the fighting arms. His company commander was Maj. D.T. 'Punch' Cowan (6th Gurkha Rifles) under whom he would serve later in Burma during World War II and earn his Military Cross. His first report from Maj. Cowan read, '… he can maintain a stiff upper lip in adversity, does not lose heart and possesses the power of command, drive and a cheerful personality. He is popular with his fellow cadets.'

As a GC, Sam displayed all the hallmarks of leadership. He stood head and shoulders above his peers and was rewarded with the rank of corporal. He excelled at most sports and was a Tennis Blue.[5] Sam was also a good boxer and loved a good fight, both inside and outside the ring. Unfortunately, horse riding, compulsory at the academy, was not his strongest suit. He always poked fun at the sport by saying, 'Never stand in front of a senior officer or behind a horse, they are both unpredictable and you never know when they will kick.'

At Amritsar railway station, Hormusji and Sheroo being seen off by Surinder Singh, Mrs Boga and Devraj Suri after one of their annual visits
Courtesy: The Manekshaw family

---

3 School Leaving Examination, currently known as 'O' Levels.
4 Telecommunications.
5 Tennis Champion: The term 'Blue' comes from a Blue Blazer which is earned by the Champion in each field of sport at the IMA.

The dispensary in the able
hands of Mr Suri
Courtesy: The Manekshaw family

*Sam was also
a good boxer
and loved a
good fight,
both inside
and outside
the ring*

What Sam did not excel in was staying out of hot waters. On 'liberty'[6] one weekend, along with two coursemates, he decided to visit the neighbouring hill station of Mussoorie. The three young men went to a floor show on Sunday evening at Hakman's Grand Hotel, lost track of time, missed the last bus to Dehradun and had to spend the night in Mussoorie. They returned to the IMA on Monday morning and were promptly marched up to the adjutant, Capt. J.F.S. McLaren of the Black Watch Regiment, on charges of truancy. As a punishment all three were gated and confined to barracks for fifteen days. Sam was stripped of his rank of corporal. Capt. McLaren could never have dreamt that the corporal he had 'detabbed'[7] would one day rise to become chief of the army staff and India's first field marshal! It was probably these escapades of his youth that in later years made Sam tolerant and indulgent of the foibles of his young officers.

In December 1934, along with the first batch of twenty-two Indians, 2nd Lt Sam Manekshaw was commissioned in the Indian Army. The medical profession's loss was the Indian Army's gain. Sam often regaled his officers' wives with the circumstances that destined him to join the army, adding with a twinkle in the eye, that had he been a gynaecologist instead of a general, their paths might still have crossed, albeit under very different circumstances!

---

6 'Liberty' was a 'permit' to go out of the academy for the weekend with the strict requirement to
   return before last light on Sunday.
7 Demoted.

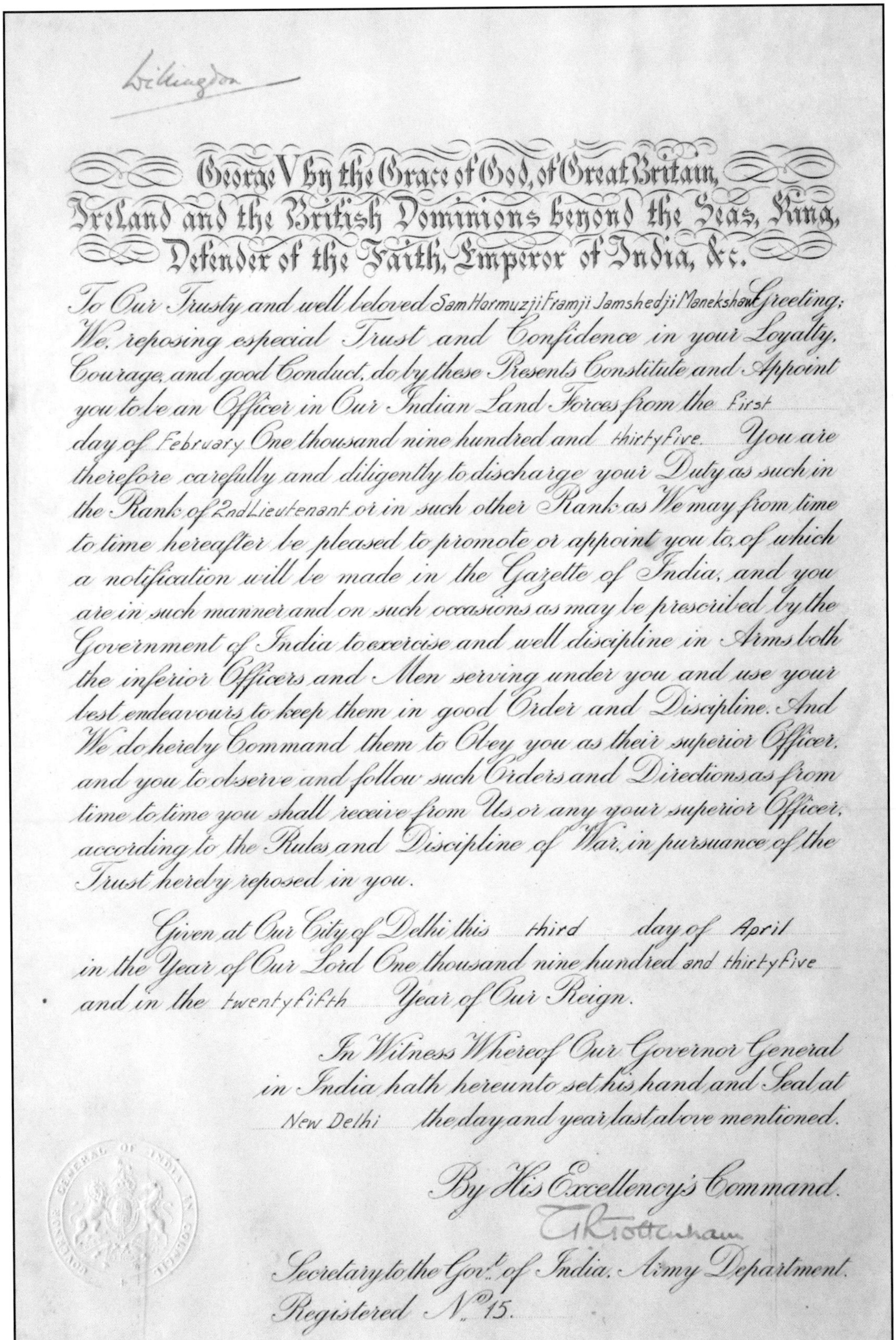

_Willingdon_

George V by the Grace of God, of Great Britain, Ireland and the British Dominions beyond the Seas, King, Defender of the Faith, Emperor of India, &c.

To Our Trusty and well beloved Sam Hormuzji Framji Jamshedji Manekshaw Greeting: We, reposing especial Trust and Confidence in your Loyalty, Courage, and good Conduct, do by these Presents Constitute and Appoint you to be an Officer in Our Indian Land Forces from the First day of February One thousand nine hundred and thirtyfive. You are therefore carefully and diligently to discharge your Duty as such in the Rank of 2nd Lieutenant or in such other Rank as We may from time to time hereafter be pleased to promote or appoint you to, of which a notification will be made in the Gazette of India, and you are in such manner and on such occasions as may be prescribed by the Government of India to exercise and well discipline in Arms both the inferior Officers and Men serving under you and use your best endeavours to keep them in good Order and Discipline. And We do hereby Command them to Obey you as their superior Officer, and you to observe and follow such Orders and Directions as from time to time you shall receive from Us or any your superior Officer, according to the Rules and Discipline of War, in pursuance of the Trust hereby reposed in you.

Given at Our City of Delhi this third day of April in the Year of Our Lord One thousand nine hundred and thirtyfive and in the twentyfifth Year of Our Reign.

In Witness Whereof Our Governor General in India hath hereunto set his hand and Seal at New Delhi the day and year last above mentioned.

By His Excellency's Command.

_T. R. Tottenham_

Secretary to the Gov.t of India, Army Department.
Registered N.o 15.

The British Commission
Courtesy: The Manekshaw family

**Visiting the clinic while on
an official tour to Amritsar**
Courtesy: The Manekshaw family

*Years went by,
but Sam's ties
with Amritsar
ran long and
deep*

Sam was a man of many talents. From his mother he inherited her sense of humour and her culinary skills. He loved to impress his guests with traditional Parsi savouries, which he had mastered by watching his mother. His penchant for pottering around the kitchen often led to confrontations with the family cook who would feign annoyance and chase him out of the kitchen, brandishing a carving knife and spewing threats. From his father he inherited his love of music and gardening. Throughout his life, his prized possession was his music system while the beautiful gardens he maintained in every house stood testimony to his green fingers.

With the announcement of Independence and Partition in August 1947, Hilla and Hormusji returned to Bombay and set up home first in Adelphi Cottage at Churchgate and later moved to Kashmir House at Breach Candy.

Hormusji's clinic with an attached pharmacy was left in the care of his trusted manager, Mr Surinder Singh, and his second pharmacy, down the road from the clinic, was left in the able hands of Mr Devraj Suri. A few years later, around 1950, Hormusji decided to gift the clinic and the pharmacies to his managers. Both men, in the spirit of reciprocity insisted on sending an annual 'allowance' to their benefactor and his wife for the rest of their lives.

Hormusji passed away in April 1964 when Sam was western army commander in Simla. After his father's death, on official visits to Bombay, Sam dispensed with all the trappings of office and spent time at home with his mother.

A few years later Hilla's health began to fail. Confined to her bed, she would lie on her side and gaze at a picture of Sam in his military regalia which she kept on her bedside table. January 15 is celebrated in India as Army Day. On this day in 1949 for the first time an Indian officer, Lt Gen. (later Field Marshal) K.M. Cariappa, was appointed commander-in-chief.[8] When Sam took over as army chief he decided he would celebrate Army Day by hosting an 'at home' for all subedar majors[9] posted in Delhi. The preparations for the party were in full swing when the phone rang. His sister Cilla had bad tidings. His mother had passed away and in accordance with Parsi custom the funeral was scheduled that evening. Sam decided to keep this news in wraps. The party proceeded as planned with him playing the cheerful, gracious host. He missed his mother's funeral.

Years went by, but Sam's ties with Amritsar ran long and deep. After he became chief, on his first official tour to Amritsar he dropped by the clinic, unannounced. Surinder Singh and Devraj Suri were ecstatic to see him. Mr Singh had kept the clinic unchanged. As a mark of respect, Hormusji's empty chair was kept in the main hall as testimony to his legacy. Word of Sam's presence spread like wildfire. Jubilant neighbours and acquaintances came to congratulate him, thronged the clinic and overflowed into the street.

After victory in the 1971 war with Pakistan, the citizens of Amritsar felicitated Sam at the historic Ram Bagh garden. Addressing the gathering, Sam said he was proud to belong to the city and happy to be amongst the people with whom he had spent the best years of his life. ◆

**Adelphi Annex and the family Citroen**
Courtesy: The Manekshaw family

---

8 Commander-in-chief was the term used for the army chief in pre-independent India.
9 Equivalent of a warrant officer.

Gentleman Cadet
Sam Manekshaw
Courtesy: The Manekshaw family

# The Young Officer

On February 4, 1934, 2nd Lt Sam Hormusji Framji Jamshedji Manekshaw, IC-14,[1] was commissioned into the army with the first batch of Indian Commissioned Officers (ICOs). This illustrious first course produced three army chiefs for the Indian subcontinent: Gen. Sam Manekshaw of India, Gen. Muhammad Musa of Pakistan and Gen. Smith Dun of Burma. Another eminent Indian from the first course was 2nd Lt Melville de Mellow of 5/2 Punjab Regiment. Melville quit the army to join All India Radio. For many years his was the deep baritone voice that wafted over the airwaves whenever the nation had occasion to rejoice or to mourn.

How did Sam come to acquire such an exceptionally long name? His adjutant at the IMA was Capt. J.F.S. McLaren. Sam was impressed with the three initials and, not to be outdone, he added the names of his father, grandfather and great-grandfather to his name. For the first year of service Sam was attached to the 2nd Battalion of the Royal Scots based in Lahore. In the good old days, subalterns were not addressed by their rank but merely as 'Mister'; you had to 'earn your spurs', so to speak. Since his name was a tongue-twister, British officers decided to nickname him Mr Macintosh! He had no option but to grin and bear it.

At the end of a year's attachment, in 1935 Sam earned his first ACR.[2] Smartly turned out with Sam Browne and sword he entered the adjutant's office. After a searing examination, he was given a dressing down. 'You are going to see the colonel? Look at you! Your bloody strap is filthy, dirty. Look at your belt, it is disgusting. Go on, go and get dressed.' Sam walked out of the adjutant's office, waited for five minutes and without as much as flicking the dust off his epaulettes, returned. He was pronounced 'much better'. After checking to see if he had a fountain pen to sign the report, the adjutant instructed, 'The CO[3] will read your report after which you will initial at the bottom left-hand corner. Is that understood?' Sam replied in the affirmative. He entered the CO's office and saluted, 'Mr Manekshaw reporting, Sir.' The CO looked Sam up and down and thrust the report at him. It was a one-liner, 'This officer, I beg your pardon, this man may someday become an officer.' Sam initialled it as he had been instructed to, and walked out. Khalid Sheikh, another

---

1 Each officer who is commissioned from the IMA gets a personal identification number which remains unchanged throughout his career.
2 Annual Confidential Report.
3 Commanding officer.

LEFT TO RIGHT:
Sam as a young subaltern
(at extreme right) on
attachment with the
Royal Scots
Courtesy: 58 Gorkha Training Centre

Sam with 4/12 FFR
somewhere in the NWFP

At home on a spot of leave
Courtesy: The Manekshaw family

officer from his regiment got a similar one-liner, 'This officer tends to be irresponsible.' The previous year Khalid's report had said he was irresponsible, so this was measured improvement!

After the year's attachment with the Royal Scots was over, Sam was posted to the 4th Battalion of the 12th Frontier Force Regiment (4/12 FFR). This battalion had been raised after the First Sikh War in 1846 as the 4th Sikh Local Infantry. In 1903 it became 54 Sikh (Frontier Force) and another reorganisation in 1922 saw its name changed once again to 4/12 FFR. Since the battalion's operational role was along the frontier of the newly acquired territories of the Punjab, it was called the Punjab Irregular Frontier Force (PIFF) and officers and men who belonged to the Frontier Force were known as PIFFERs. The class composition of the 4/12 FFR was a mix of Sikhs and Pashtuns.[4] According to the traditions of the British Indian Army, followed by the Indian Army to this day, officers are expected to speak the language of the soldiers they command. Sam was fluent in Punjabi, the language of the Sikhs, and in a short order he mastered Pashto, the language of the Pashtuns. In fact, with his sharp features and his light-coloured eyes Sam was often mistaken for one!

This boyishly handsome officer was assigned to a Sikh platoon but his fair skin and rather delicate features did not quite impress the sturdy Sikhs. One day he overheard them lamenting their fate, 'Oi kurri nu platoon commander bana ditta. Hun ki kariye!' (What shall we do now that a girl

---

4 Pashtuns (or Pathans) are tribesmen from the North West Frontier region of Pakistan.

has been made our platoon commander!) Sam walked away silently, determined to make them eat their words. A few days later, on his way to play tennis, Sam passed his platoon athletes practising the high jump. The ace athlete struggled repeatedly but could not clear a four-foot bar. Racquet in hand, with a short run, Sam sailed over the bar and turning to the men, he said in Punjabi, *'Tusi keho jaye athlete ho! Aina ucha te kudyian wi tap jandiya ne.'* (What kind of athletes are you? Even girls can easily jump over this bar.) The soldiers fell silent; little did they know that their platoon commander had been raised in Amritsar and spoke fluent Punjabi. A week later Sam took another calculated risk and beat his ace platoon runner after giving him a lead. He had unequivocally established his credentials and the men readily accepted him as their leader.[5]

In 1939 Sam married Silloo Bode and in 1940 their daughter, Sherry, was born. 4/12 FFR was mostly stationed in the NWFP to contain tribal insurgency. This was a field posting, and his young family had to stay back in Amritsar with his parents.

In 1942, with the outbreak of World War II and the Japanese invasion of Burma, 4/12 FFR was deployed along the Sittang river. Sam was a captain, commanding 'A' Company. The Japanese had attacked and captured Pagoda hill, a strategic position. On February 22 he was ordered to launch a counter-attack. Along with his company officer, 2nd Lt Mohammed Attique 'Turk'

---

5 As narrated by Maj. Gen. K.S. Bajwa.

*Sam was hit by a burst of LMG fire that lodged nine bullets in his abdomen and perforated his lungs, liver, kidneys and intestines*

*Sam ... would joke that his abdomen was made of steel that Japanese bullets could not smash*

Rahman, who later rose to the rank of lieutenant general in the Pakistan Army, he recaptured the position, but the company suffered heavy casualties. Sam was hit by a burst of LMG[6] fire that lodged nine bullets in his abdomen and perforated his lungs, liver, kidneys and intestines. Fearing that carrying the wounded would dangerously slow down withdrawal of the battalion, the commanding officer ordered all casualties to be left behind. The senior subedar[7] of Sam's company protested vehemently, *'Sam Sahib tey sadi company da sartaj aye. Asi ohnu pichhe kiven chhad sakde hain.'* (Sam Sahib is the honoured head of our company. How can we leave him behind?) This was an extraordinary tribute to the young officer's leadership. Sam's orderly, Sher Singh, carried him on his back to the Medical Aid Post which was choking with the wounded and urged the doctors to attend to Sam, but to no avail. In desperation this simple and loyal soldier threatened the doctor with his loaded rifle, saying, *'Asi Japanian de nal larde hue wi apne sahib nun milan tak chuk ke le ke aiye han. Hun asi apne sahib nun mardian nahin dekh sakde. Sahib ji, tusin ehnan da ilaj karo nahin te mainun goli chalaunin pai gi.'* (We have carried our revered leader for miles while fighting against the Japanese. We are not going to see him die now

6 Light Machine Gun.
7 A subedar is a rank in the Indian Army, ranking below commissioned officers and above non-commissioned officers.

**The Illustrious First Course. Sam is fourth from left in the top row**
Courtesy: Anandale Museum

THE COMMANDANT WITH THE FIRST BATCH OF GCs TO PASS OUT FRO
THE INDIAN MILITARY ACADEMY - DECEMBER 1934

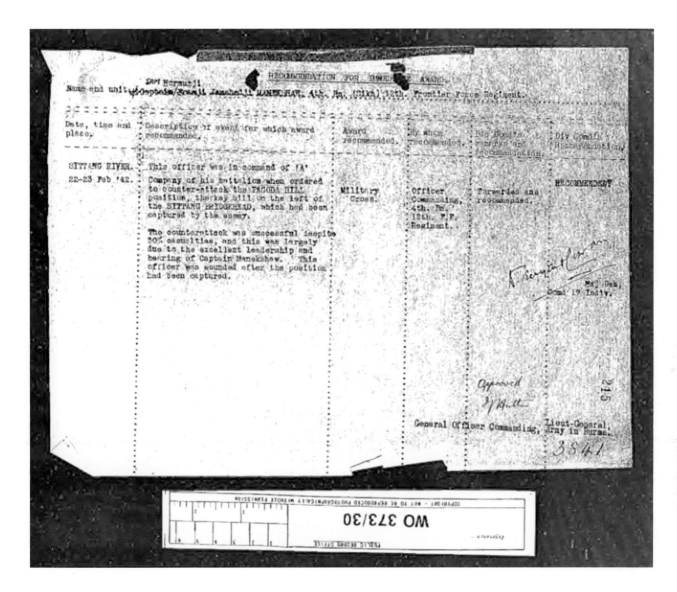

RECOMMENDATION FOR IMMEDIATE AWARD

Name and unit: Captain/Brevet Jamshedji MANEKSHAW, 4th. Bn. (SIKH) 12th. Frontier Force Regiment.

| Date, time and place. | Description of event for which award recommended. | Award recommended. | By whom recommended. | Bde. Comdr's remarks and recommendation. | Div Comdr's Recommendation. |
|---|---|---|---|---|---|
| SITTANG RIVER. 22-23 Feb '42. | This officer was in command of 'A' Company of his battalion when ordered to counter-attack the PAGODA HILL position, thereby hill on the left of the SITTANG BRIDGEHEAD, which had been captured by the enemy.<br><br>The counterattack was successful inspite 50% casulties, and this was largely due to the excellent leadership and bearing of Captain Manekshaw. This officer was wounded after the position had been captured. | Military Cross. | Officer Commanding, 4th. Bn. 12th. F.F. Regiment. | Forwarded and recommended. | RECOMMENDED<br><br>*signature*<br>Maj. Gen.<br>Comd 17 Indiv. |

Approved
*signature*

General Officer Commanding, Lieut-General, Army in Burma.

3841

WO 373/30

COPYRIGHT 1941 - NOT TO BE REPRODUCED PHOTOGRAPHICALLY WITHOUT PERMISSION

PUBLIC RECORD OFFICE

because you are not attending to him. Please sir, treat him or I will be forced to shoot you.) The doctor attended to Sam, albeit reluctantly, for he merely removed the bullets and some length of perforated intestines and sutured him in a slipshod manner, leaving a slight but permanent bulge in his abdomen. After surgery, Sam was convalescing in the military hospital in Pegu when it came under aerial bombardment. Along with other patients, he was evacuated first to Mandalay, then to Rangoon and finally to India on the last troopship that sailed from that port before it fell to the Japanese. Sam owed his life to his orderly, Sher Singh, and he never allowed himself to forget that. Recounting his near brush with death he would joke that his abdomen was made of steel that Japanese bullets could not smash.

The young captain had fought valiantly and his chances of survival seemed slim. From the battlefield his commanding officer and his brigade commander dispatched a signal to higher headquarters, recommending that he be awarded the Military Cross (MC). Maj. Gen. Cowan,

Recommendation for
Military Cross
Courtesy: The National Archives, UK

**Silloo, the demure damsel**
Courtesy: The Manekshaw family

Sam's company commander at the IMA, was GOC[8] 17 Infantry Division. He promptly endorsed the recommendation since a Military Cross cannot be awarded posthumously. It has often been said that the general took off his own medal and pinned it on Sam's chest. This is a myth as medals are not worn during combat operations. The citation was approved and the young captain became a decorated officer.

From 1943–1946 Sam moved every few months. From August 23 to December 22, 1943 he attended the 8th Staff College Course at Quetta (now in Pakistan). It was here that he established an enduring friendship with his DS,[9] Maj. J.N. 'Muchu' Chaudhuri, who became the chief of the army staff in 1962. Sam had been promoted to the rank of major. He performed well during the course and on completion, in January 1944, he was posted as BM[10] Razmak Brigade, North Waziristan (now in Pakistan). WWII was still raging and ten months later, in October, he was ordered to report to 9/12 FFR in Burma under Gen. W.J. Slim's 14th Army. In 1945 he was back at the Staff College in Quetta as a DS, the first ICO to hold this appointment. It was during this tenure that his second daughter, Maja, was born. WWII was drawing to a close and in November 1945 Sam was posted as staff officer to Gen. Daisy in Indo-China (now Vietnam) to assist with the rehabilitation of over 10,000 Japanese POWs.

Sam's organisational skills and his qualities of leadership had caught the attention of the commander-in-chief, Field Marshal Lord Claude Auchinleck. In March 1946 he was selected to join an Indian military delegation on a six-month lecture tour of Australia, the main purpose of which was to highlight India's achievements during WWII.

---

8 General Officer Commanding.
9 In military colleges the term DS or Directing Staff is used for instructors whose role is to conduct and direct discussions rather than to instruct.
10 A brigade major is like the chief of staff to a brigadier, responsible for all operations.

On his return from Australia in September Sam was promoted to lieutenant colonel and posted to the General Headquarters[11] as GSO1 in the Military Operations Directorate-3 (MO-3), responsible for perspective planning. In 1946 very few Indian officers had attained the rank of lieutenant colonel; by all indications Sam had a promising career ahead of him. Soon thereafter Maj. A.M. Yahya Khan was posted as GSO2 in MO-1 Directorate, responsible for the NWFP and Waziristan, and Capt. S.K. Sinha was appointed GSO3 in MO-2 Directorate that dealt with internal security. For the first time three Indians were posted in a directorate which until then had been a British bastion. At the time of Partition, Maj. Yahya Khan opted for Pakistan. By a strange quirk of destiny, at the time of the 1971 Indo-Pak war, Sam and Yahya had risen to become chiefs of their respective armies and were ranged on opposing sides. Meanwhile, Capt. S.K. Sinha became a lieutenant general and served as vice chief of the Indian Army from 1981–1983. After retirement he was appointed as ambassador to Nepal (1990–1991), governor of Assam (1997–2003) and governor of Jammu and Kashmir (2003–2008). ◆

LEFT TO RIGHT:
**Sam with his firstborn, Sherry**

**With his second born, Maja**
Courtesy: The Manekshaw family

---

11 Army Headquarters was known as General Headquarters during the Raj.

Lieutenant Colonel
Sam Manekshaw
Courtesy: The Manekshaw family

# Independence and Partition

On February 20, 1947, the British government announced its decision to grant independence to India. The euphoria was short-lived for on June 3 it was decreed that the country was to be divided into the two sovereign nations of India and Pakistan. This meant not just drawing new boundaries but distribution of assets, including those of the army. On June 16 the Armed Forces Reconstitution Committee was formed. It directed that two-thirds of all physical assets would remain with India and one-third would be apportioned to Pakistan. Regiments, units and sub-units with Muslim majority troops would be assigned to the Pakistan Army while Hindu and Sikh regiments would remain with the Indian Army. This was a Herculean task. Teams worked overtime to separate the files of military establishments and the service records of personnel that would soon belong to the new state of Pakistan. Even more challenging was the redistribution of operational plans. In March itself when there were indications that the country would be partitioned, Sam's directorate, MO-3, began sorting maps and plans of territories that would become part of Pakistan from those that would remain with India, except that operational plans are not made in isolation. In a brilliant move, to keep the records complete, Sam had the foresight to get copies made of all material marked for Pakistan.

D-Day dawned. The parting was gut-wrenching as officers from the same regiment, whose ties are often stronger than family bonds, prepared to go their separate ways. On August 14, 1947, Indian officers hosted a farewell at the Delhi Gymkhana Club for their comrades who would soon leave for Pakistan. The evening was marked with bonhomie and promises to remain in touch and with varied renditions of 'Auld Lang Syne' and 'He's a Jolly Good Fellow'. A silver trophy with a Hindu and a Muslim soldier, both training their guns at a common enemy, was presented by Maj. Gen. K.M. Cariappa, the senior-most Indian officer, to Brig. A.M. Raza, the senior-most Pakistani officer. No one present that evening could have foreseen the tragedy that the guns would soon be trained at each other!

Pakistan and India became independent nations on August 14 and 15, 1947, respectively. On August 17 the British unveiled the border, the Radcliffe Line, drawn by Sir Cyril Radcliffe, that now divided the two countries. This triggered a mass migration of ten to twelve million people as Muslims from India moved to their new homeland, Pakistan, while Hindus and Sikhs from what was

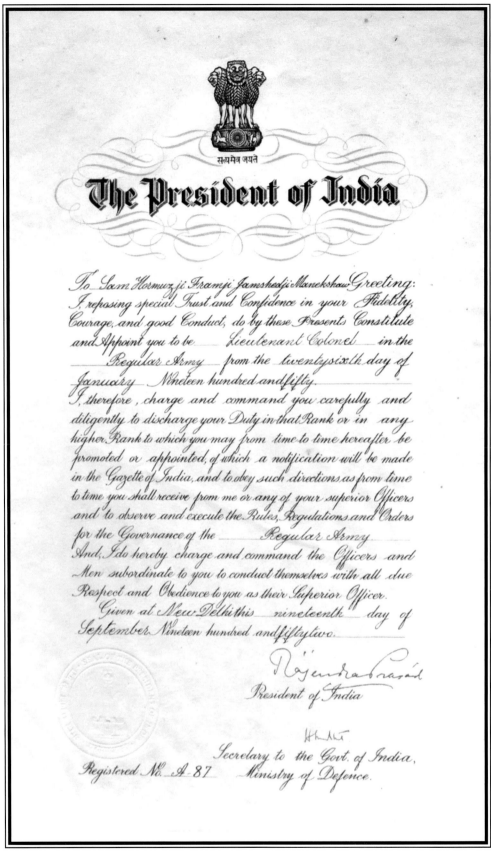

The President of India

To Sam Hormuz ji Framji Jamshedji Manekshaw Greeting: I, reposing special Trust and Confidence in your Fidelity, Courage, and good Conduct, do by these Presents Constitute and Appoint you to be Lieutenant Colonel in the Regular Army from the twentysixth day of January Nineteen hundred and fifty.

I, therefore, charge and command you carefully and diligently to discharge your Duty in that Rank or in any higher Rank to which you may from time to time hereafter be promoted or appointed, of which a notification will be made in the Gazette of India, and to obey such directions as from time to time you shall receive from me or any of your superior Officers and to observe and execute the Rules, Regulations and Orders for the Governance of the Regular Army And, I do hereby charge and command the Officers and Men subordinate to you to conduct themselves with all due Respect and Obedience to you as their Superior Officer.

Given at New Delhi this nineteenth day of September Nineteen hundred and fiftytwo.

Rajendra Prasad
President of India

Secretary to the Govt. of India,
Registered No. A-87    Ministry of Defence.

**FACING PAGES:**
Presidential Order to Indian officers when India became a Republic in English and Hindi
Courtesy: 58 Gorkha Training Centre

सत्यमेव जयते

# भारत का राष्ट्रपति

साम होर्मुज्जी फ्रामजी जमशेदजी मानेकशा को स्वस्तिवचन, में, आपकी बफादारी, साहस और सदाचार में विशेष आस्था और विश्वास करके इन उपहारों द्वारा आपको स्थायी सेना में लैफ्टिनेंट कर्नल कोटि में सन १९५० के जनवरी मास के छब्बीसवें दिवस से प्रतिष्ठित और नियुक्त करता हूं ।

अतएव में आपको यह प्रभार और आदेश देता हूं कि आप अपनी इस कोटि में के या इससे उच्चतर किसी कोटि में के जिस पर समय समय पर एतत् पश्चात् आप पदोन्नत या नियुक्त हों जिसकी सूचना भारत के गज़ट में दी जायगी अपने कर्तव्यों का सावधानी और श्रम-शीलता से पालन करें और मुझसे या अपने किसी उच्चतर पदधारी से मिलनेवाले निर्देशों को मानें तथा स्थायी सेना के शासन सम्बन्धी नियमों, विनियमों और आदेशों का पालन और निष्पादन करते रहें ।

तथा में आपके मातहत पदधारियों और आदमियों को यह प्रभार और आदेश एतत् द्वारा देता हूं कि बे आपका अपने उच्चतर पदधारी के रूप में आदर और आज्ञानुवर्तन करें ।

सन १९५२ के सितम्बर मास के आज उन्नीसवें दिवस को नई दिल्ली में प्रदत्त ।

*राजेन्द्र प्रसाद*

भारत का राष्ट्रपति

*एच एम पटेल*

प्रतिरक्षा मंत्रालय में भारत सरकार
का सचिव

पंजीयन संख्या ९-९७

now Pakistan, left for India. Emotions ran high in the Punjab as the displaced were forced to leave their homes, their wealth and the land they had tilled for generations. This resulted in the outbreak of communal frenzy and riots. The backlash was difficult to contain and spilt into Delhi as hordes of refugees, bitter and indigent, poured into the city. The army was called out. MO Directorate had to assist the civil administration in maintaining law and order. Sam burnt the midnight oil, working closely with Mr H.M. Patel, officer-in-charge of the Emergency Committee for administering Delhi.

Another issue of Partition that needed to be settled related to the 565 princely states ruled by maharajas. The British in their wisdom had given the maharajas autonomy to govern their states as long as they acknowledged the suzerainty of the crown. These states were not officially part of the British Empire and therefore, at the time of Independence, the maharajas were required to opt for India or Pakistan by signing an 'Instrument of Accession'. In 1947 Sardar Vallabhbhai Patel was deputy prime minister and held the additional appointment of 'Minister of (princely) States'. V.P. Menon was secretary in the ministry. He was directed by the Sardar to visit each state, accompanied by Sam and secure their accession. Sam describes himself as the 'bogeyman … who made it all happen'. In most cases accession was not an issue. A vast majority of the princely states were surrounded by Indian territory and by August 14 most of them had opted for India with the exception of J&K, Junagadh in Kathiawar district and Hyderabad in the Deccan. Initially, the nawab of Junagadh opted for Pakistan. This was a provocative political move which was not sustainable as the state was fenced in by Indian territory. With the intervention of Lord Mountbatten and pressure from other princely states of Kathiawar, the decision was rescinded and Junagadh acceded to India in early November 1947 while the nawab fled to Pakistan with his family and the crown jewels. The Nizam of Hyderabad sought independence for his state but was informed by Lord Mountbatten that this was not an option. In spite of that Hyderabad held out until a small military operation on September 13, 1948 saw its accession to India.

The situation in J&K[1] posed an altogether unique challenge with a Muslim majority in the valley, a Hindu majority in Jammu, a Buddhist majority in Ladakh, a Hindu ruler and a border contiguous with Pakistan to the west and India to the south. While the Muslim population in the valley was an overriding majority, the strain of Islam practised by Kashmiri Muslims was a syncretic theology rooted in Sufism and distinctly different from the Islam practised in other parts of the subcontinent. The political leader of the valley, Sheikh Abdullah, was strongly opposed to the idea of partition based on religion and preferred to remain with secular India. The ruler, Maharaja Hari Singh, was in a quandary. To complicate matters, on October 22, 1947 Pakistani 'raiders' (irregular troops), comprising mostly tribesmen from NWFP, followed by regular units of the Pakistan Army, incognito, a charge denied by Pakistan for many months, began closing in on Srinagar with the objective of occupying Kashmir. En route, the tribesmen indulged in plunder, rape and massacre, destroying the towns of Baramulla, Rajouri and Poonch.

*Lord Mountbatten ... turned to Sam and said, ' … Manekji [he always got his name wrong], what is the military situation?'*

---

1 The information in this section on the accession of J&K, including the cabinet meeting and the mobilisation of troops has been sourced from *The Origins of a Dispute: Kashmir 1947* (New Edition) by Prem Shankar Jha.

They killed Col. Tom Dykes of the Sikh Regiment and his wife, who were holidaying in Kashmir. Sam was upset since he and Tom had done their attachment with the Royal Scots at the same time. When Muzaffarabad and Domel fell to the raiders, a desperate maharaja turned to India for protection. His state forces were no match for the Pakistan Army. Some of them, being Muslim, had joined hands with the raiders. But military support from India was predicated on his signing the Instrument of Accession, else it could be considered an act of aggression.

On October 25 at 2.30 pm, Chief of General Staff, Lt Gen. Sir Roy Bucher, walked into Sam's office and ordered him to accompany V.P. Menon to Srinagar. Sam was deputy Director Military Operations (DMO) at the time. By 4.00 pm the team was airborne in an IAF[2] Dakota, with Squadron Leader Hari Chand Dewan (later air marshal and AOC-in-C[3] Eastern Air Command during the 1971 war) at the controls. Menon was to secure the maharaja's accession while Sam was to assess the military situation. Sam recalls that the palace was in total disarray. Priceless

**With General Sir Roy Bucher**
Courtesy: The Manekshaw family

jewels and treasures lay strewn everywhere while servants packed and loaded trucks that lined the driveway in preparation for imminent departure to Jammu. The maharaja was visibly distressed and incoherent. He turned to Sam and threatened to lead his state forces to battle the marauding tribesmen if Delhi did not send in the army. Sam later said that he could barely contain himself from saying, 'Sure that will raise their morale, Sir!' Menon prevailed and in the early hours of October 26 the maharaja signed the Instrument of Accession. With that the state of J&K officially joined the Dominion of India. Meanwhile, Sam was able to determine from officers of the J&K state forces that the raiders were seven to nine kilometres from Srinagar airport. It was imperative to return to Delhi urgently and mobilise the army, but Srinagar did not have night flying facilities. Local officials and politicians lit the runway with pine torches and the Dakota with Sam and V.P. Menon on board lifted off for Delhi. Mission accomplished!

From the airport Sam went directly to Gen. Bucher's residence and apprised him of the urgency of the situation. The general told him to accompany him to a meeting of the Defence Committee of the Cabinet to be held later that morning at the Viceregal Lodge[4] and present his assessment. After Nehru, Sardar Patel and other cabinet ministers had settled down, Menon handed over the Instrument of Accession to Lord Mountbatten who turned to Sam and said, '… Manekji [he always got his name wrong], what is the military situation?' Sam briefed the committee. The raiders were only a few kilometres away from Srinagar. It was end-October and

2 Indian Air Force.
3 Air Officer Commanding-in-Chief.
4 The Viceroy's residence, which today is the Rashtrapati Bhavan.

To Sam, one of the best staff officers I
have ever met

14th January, 1949.
Roy Bucher, General
C-in-C, Indian Army

with the first snowfall access to Kashmir would close till spring. The only road linking India to Kashmir was through the Banihal pass at a height of 9,300 feet across the Pir Panjal range. There was no Jawahar tunnel until 1956. Srinagar airport had a fair-weather grass airfield that also closed in winter due to snow, rendering Kashmir inaccessible by road or by air till the snow melted in April or May. Time was of the essence. If troops were not flown in immediately, the tribesmen would descend into the valley, secure the airport, seal off entry by India, and Kashmir would be lost for good. The committee looked to Prime Minister Nehru for a decision. Nehru hesitated. He was concerned about world opinion and talked about consulting the United Nations until an impatient Sardar Patel wrested the initiative from him. 'Jawahar, do you want Kashmir or do you want to give it away?' 'Of course, I want Kashmir,' was Nehru's indignant response. The Sardar turned to Sam and said, 'You have your marching orders.' At 11.00 am on October 26 the airlift commenced from Delhi's Safdarjung airport with six IAF aircraft and fifty Dakotas that had been requisitioned a few days earlier from private airlines. A total of 800 sorties were flown for a fortnight. By November 16 the raiders had been repulsed from the valley and Srinagar and the airport were secured although engagement with the infiltrators in the rest of Kashmir and along the border continued for another fourteen months.

It is of interest to note that the Pakistan Commander-in-Chief (C-in-C), Gen. Sir Frank Walter Messervy, had informed his Indian counterpart, Gen. Sir Robert Lockhart, of the impending infiltration by the raiders. For reasons best known to him, Lockhart chose to keep the Indian government in the dark and took no preventive action. When Sardar Patel got to know of this Lockhart was sacked on grounds of disloyalty and Lt Gen. Sir Roy Bucher was appointed C-in-C on December 31, 1947. Bucher held Sam in very high regard.

With Partition, Sam's 4/12 FFR was assigned to Pakistan and he found himself rudderless without a parent unit. With a heavy heart he gave up wearing the shoulder titles and silver badges of rank worn by 'PIFFERs'. Initially he was empanelled on the strength of 16 Punjab Regiment but in December 1947 he was ordered to take over command of the 3rd Battalion of the 5th Gorkha Rifles (3/5 GR) since the 5th Gorkha Rifles was also part of the 'PIFFERs' group. On receiving this news Sam rejoiced and promptly donned the black shoulder titles and the red lanyard of 5 GR. In Bombay the battalion geared up to welcome their new commanding officer. The adjutant, Capt. (later Major General) F.L. 'Freddie' Freemantle, went to Santa Cruz railway station to receive the new CO. The train arrived but there was no sign of Sam. Freddie paced the platform for a while and then returned to the battalion to be handed a signal that had just arrived from Delhi informing him that Sam's posting had been cancelled. The Kashmir issue had escalated and the C-in-C, Gen. Sir Roy Bucher, could not afford to change his deputy DMO at this juncture. For an infantry officer commanding a battalion is the highlight of his career. Sam never commanded a battalion, a regret he nursed throughout his life.

With turmoil in the country MO-3 worked round the clock. During these tense and action-filled days it was Sam's sense of humour that lightened up the sombre atmosphere. In the services, medals and ribbons are worn in order of seniority. Gen. S.K. Sinha recollects Sam joking that

*'To Sam, one of the best staff officers I have ever met.' Roy Bucher, General*

**ABOVE:**
Sam as a young officer
with FFR

**RIGHT ABOVE:**
Military Cross

**RIGHT BELOW:**
Independence medal
Courtesy: Center for Armed
Forces Historical Research

King George VI must be very unhappy since the Jai Hind[5] (Independence) medal had displaced the Military Cross! Sam was referring to the newly issued directive by the government whereby medals awarded by independent India took precedence over British medals.

In 1948 Sam was promoted to colonel and in April that year he and Maj. Gen. Thimayya (Timmy) were deputed to accompany an Indian delegation headed by Sir B.N. Rau, an eminent jurist, to a UN conference on Kashmir to be held in Paris. Sam with his MO Directorate experience and 'Timmy' in his capacity as GOC 19 Infantry Division, Baramulla (Kashmir), were military advisors to the delegation. Sam boarded the ship in Bombay to find that a fellow passenger was the young Indira Gandhi who was headed to Europe on a personal trip. During the voyage they established an instant rapport, a rapport that would serve them and the nation well in the future.

As an outcome of the conference, UN Resolution 47 was passed on April 21, 1948. It first called on Pakistan to withdraw all tribesmen and non-Kashmiris from the occupied territories in Kashmir and to desist from providing material aid to the fighters. It then called on India to

---

5 *Jai Hind* literally means 'glory to India'. It is a commonly used salutation.

take the second step of a staged withdrawal of forces, and at stage three, conduct a free and fair plebiscite. The first step was never taken by Pakistan and hostilities continued all through 1948 until a ceasefire was ordered at midnight on December 31. Sam, who had been promoted to the acting rank of brigadier, was Director, MO. He signed the signal for ceasefire on behalf of the C-in-C, Gen. Bucher, albeit reluctantly, for the raiders had captured the north-western part of Kashmir. With the declaration of ceasefire, the Indian Army was asked to stop in its tracks just when it was poised to evict the tribesmen and reclaim all of Kashmir. India calls this captured territory Pakistan Occupied Kashmir (POK), while Pakistan refers to it as Azad (free) Jammu and Kashmir (AJK). For Sam, December 31, 1948 would always spell 'the tragic day of no return'.

Gen. Sir Roy Bucher retired on January 14, 1949 and Gen. K.M. Cariappa succeeded him as the first Indian C-in-C on January 15. In the month of July the UNCIP[6] convened a meeting in Karachi to delineate the Ceasefire Line, a military 'boundary'. The Indian delegation was headed by Lt Gen. Shrinagesh, GOC-in-C[7] Western Command, and comprised of Maj. Gen. K.S. Thimayya, GOC 19 Infantry Division and Brig. Sam Manekshaw, DMO. By a strange coincidence all three members of this delegation became chiefs of the Indian Army. The Pakistani delegation was led by Maj. Gen. R. Cawthorn, deputy chief of staff, and comprised of Maj. Gen. Nazir Ahmed, GOC 9 Infantry Division at Muzaffarabad (POK) and Brig. Sher Khan, DMO. Thimayya and Nazir had been coursemates at Sandhurst and were commanding opposing divisions. On July 27, 1949, the Karachi Agreement was ratified. The Ceasefire Line (CFL) was demarcated from the Rann of Kutch in Gujarat in the south to Kashmir, upto '... Chalunka (on the Shyok River), Khor and thence to the glaciers.'[8] Beyond Khor the alignment was vague for in 1949 no one visualised that the jagged heights and glacial region of Siachen would become a theatre of conflict thirty-five years later. ◆

*During these tense and action-filled days it was Sam's sense of humour that lightened up the sombre atmosphere*

6 United Nations Commission for India and Pakistan.
7 General Officer Commanding-in-Chief.
8 See: http://www.kashmirlife.net/karachi-agreement, reference para B, 2 (iii) (d).

As colonel of the regiment,
at a parade at 58 Gorkha
Training Centre

FACING PAGE:
Inspecting troops of 5/8
GR during a ceremonial
parade
Courtesy: 58 Gorkha Training Centre

# The Brigadier and Major General

In March 1952 Sam was posted to Ferozepur in the Punjab to command 167 Infantry Brigade. Ferozepur used to be a key military outpost through which the British controlled the NWFP. Post-independence, it retained its strategic importance for two reasons: it is a border town, twelve kilometres from Pakistan on the southern bank of the river Sutlej, which is a vital water source to support its agrarian economy. Although operational commitments in Ferozepur were demanding, for the first time in many years Sam was able to do some peacetime soldiering and enjoy a slower-paced life that an army cantonment had to offer. His green fingers and the alluvial soil of Ferozepur district ensured that Brigade House[1] was always a riot of colours while a vegetable patch ensured a supply of fresh greens. Sam even experimented with growing cotton, a staple of Ferozepur district. The Manekshaws were a popular couple at the army club. Sam enjoyed an occasional game of bridge, and picnics along the banks of the Sutlej were a favourite outing. Finally, Sam took some time out for his family.

---

1 Official residence of the brigade commander.

When Sam was in Ferozepur, 2/8 GR was also located in the station. Though they were not part of his brigade, Sam was a frequent guest at battalion functions. The 'Johnny'[2] Gorkhas instantly took to him as he to them. He admired their forthrightness and their bravery and was known to have said, 'Anyone who says he knows no fear is either a liar or a Gorkha.'

On May 24, 1953 Sam was appointed colonel of the regiment of 8th Gorkha Rifles, an appointment he held for two decades till he relinquished office in 1973. In this capacity he frequently visited 8 GR battalions. During one such visit to 6/8 GR Sam accosted a rifleman on guard duty, *'Mero nam ke ho?'* (What is my name— more like, do you recognise me?) Without hesitation the Johnny pronounced him 'Sam Bahadur', adding the standard Gorkha suffix of 'bahadur' or brave to his first name. The response was spontaneous and brilliant and earned the Johnny a *'thuloo rakshi'* (a large peg of rum) that evening.[3] Sam loved the sobriquet and it was what he came to be known by in the army. In 1987 Subedar Maj. L.B. Gurung (8 GR), Director of Music, Military Music Wing, composed a quick march, 'Sam Bahadur', as a tribute to the grand old man of the army.

Sam at a brigade function in Ferozepur. Silloo, in a white saree, is seated on the adjacent sofa to the left
Courtesy: 58 Gorkha Training Centre

With two years behind him in Ferozepur, in April 1954 Sam was back at Army Headquarters, this time as officiating Director, Military Training (DMT). Barely had he completed eight months and in January 1955 he was appointed the first Indian commandant of the Infantry School at Mhow. Sam arrived in Mhow on a Saturday and on Sunday morning he drove to the army club, known in those days as the Club of Central India, to make some purchases at its very popular bakery. He had barely parked his car in the porch and taken a few steps when a young officer accosted him and told him to move his car to the parking lot, explaining that parking in the porch was the prerogative of the commandant alone. Sam apologised profusely, complied with the instructions, made his purchases and drove home. On Monday morning staff and students of the Infantry School assembled in the auditorium to welcome the new commandant and listen to his introductory address. As soon as the speech was delivered, a highly agitated Maj. Adi Sethna of Rajputana Rifles, who later rose to the rank of lieutenant general and retired as the vice chief of the army, rushed to the commandant and apologised for the faux pas he had committed the previous day. Sam enjoyed Adi's discomfort for a few minutes before he brushed it off with a laugh!

2 A common term used for Gorkha soldiers.
3 Sourced from the article, 'Gentlemen, There'll Be No More Retreat' by Maj. Gen. Ashok K. Mehta (2/5 GR) published in *Outlook*, July 2008.

The Infantry School used to conduct battalion, company and platoon level tactical courses and impart training on use of small arms and infantry battalion support weapons. As commandant, Sam put in long hours with the DS community to update training doctrines and manuals from British times and make them relevant to India's post-independence security environment. This was a Herculean task and the commandant and his staff burnt the midnight oil to get the task accomplished.

Lt Gen. Sinha, who was a DS at the Infantry School at the time, recalls an interesting episode, for with Sam in the saddle, there could never be a dull moment. During a sand model discussion some of the student officers, in spite of being corrected, consistently pronounced 'grove' as 'groove'. Suddenly Sam took the floor and drew a dirty picture on the blackboard to explain the difference between grove and groove. He had the entire batch of 100 student officers in splits, and 'grove' was never mispronounced thereafter.

Mhow is a cantonment township, nestled in the Malwa plateau, in the state of Madhya Pradesh in central India. Its salubrious climate and undulating landscape dotted with colonial bungalows makes it an ideal military cantonment. Life in the town was slow-paced, affordable and idyllic. The Manekshaws made friends with the local civilians, including a sizeable number of Parsis. Years later, when I was posted there in the 1970s and 1980s, first as a student and later as a DS, the mere mention of Sam's name to any of the local residents and some of the old shopkeepers would elicit cherished memories of his acts of kindness or a witty comment he had made, all of which was related with a great deal of pride and nostalgia.

In November 1956 Sam was nominated to attend a course at the Imperial Defence College (now known as the Royal College of Defence Studies) in England. Silloo and the girls accompanied him to the UK for a year.

*As commandant, Sam put in long hours with the DS community to update training doctrines and manuals from British times and make them relevant to India's post-independence security environment*

**Sam and Silloo with officers and wives of 5/8 GR**
Courtesy: 58 Gorkha Training Centre

On his return to India in December 1957 he was promoted to major general and posted to Jammu to command 26 Infantry Division which guards the southern access to the Kashmir valley. 2/8 GR, commanded by Lt Col. Kushal Singh Thapa, was part of his division, based at Akhnoor.

Because of a paucity of army accommodation few families came to Jammu and those who made the move regardless, had to reside in the city in civilian accommodation. This included the CO and his wife, Neena, who was a doctor by profession. Neena worked in the battalion's welfare centre, providing free medical services to soldiers' families. When Sam got to know of this, he requested her to look after all 'his families' in the division. He had no funds to pay her, but she was appointed 'Honorary Medical Officer' and given a jeep and a security pass so that she could travel to the border towns of Samba, Akhnoor and Nagrota where the troops were located. Neelam recalls that Sam and Silloo were highly cognizant of the hardships and frequent separations army families endured and both of them went out of their way to ensure that a minimum level of comfort was provided when they had the opportunity to live with their husbands. Sam would bake cakes and personally go to the unit lines to distribute treats to jawans'[4]

TOP:
**Rare photograph of Sam in Gorkha hat**
Courtesy: 58 Gorkha Training Centre
ABOVE:
**Bound for the UK**
Courtesy: The Manekshaw family

——————————

4 Soldiers'.

children. Silloo could always be counted on for support when any member of a soldier's family was admitted to the hospital, especially if the unit was out on training and the men were away.

As a senior officer Sam was consistently fair and balanced while dealing with the men he commanded. He knew when to let his hair down and put them at ease and where to draw the line to maintain order and discipline. The experiences of Lt Gen. J.C. Pant (Madras Regiment) serve as a pointer to these qualities. In 1957, he and two other subalterns, freshly commissioned from the IMA, were posted in Jammu. On their first weekend in station, the three young men went to the Usman Club[5] for a dinner and dance event, formally attired in dinner jackets. At the entrance to the club, on a sofa was seated an extremely handsome gentleman in an open-collar shirt in blatant defiance of protocol. Next to him was a pretty young girl. To impress the young lady, one of the officers swaggered up to the duo and addressing the gentleman said, 'On parade I'm Jagmohan Lal Bakshi of 13 Dogra Regiment, off parade I enjoy a Scotch and soda.' The gentleman was quick to repartee, 'On parade I like a Scotch and soda, off parade I command a division.' The penny did not drop and star-struck 'Jimmy' Bakshi asked the young lady for a dance. When they took to the floor she warned him to be cautious for the handsome man on the sofa was

As GOC 26 Infantry
Division, with the Band
JCO of 2/8 GR
Courtesy: 2/8 Gorkha Rifles

very jealous of anyone who danced with her. As the evening wore on, the subalterns noticed that the gentleman had made a note of their names. This ruffled their composure when discreet enquiries revealed that he was none other than their GOC and the young lady was his daughter, Sherry. Expecting their careers to end even before they had begun, they were in for a surprise when they found themselves invited to Flag Staff House[6] for cocktails. However, this invitation meant they would have some explaining to do to their commanding officers for protocol demanded that you could not accept an invitation from the GOC and keep your CO in the dark. They managed to cross that hurdle without much ado.

A few weeks later another one of the trio, 2nd Lt J.C. Pant, was caught by the military police for violating army regulations. J.C. had been ordered by his CO to go with the dispatch rider (DR)[7] and collect cash for the battalion's monthly pay (distribution) parade. The DR seemed a bit unsteady so J.C. took charge and rode the bike, with the dispatch rider sitting pillion. Unfortunately, at a TCP (Traffic Check Post) he was pulled over by the CMP (Corps of Military Police) for riding a military vehicle without authorisation, marched up to his brigade commander, Jhangoo Satarawalla, and given a severe reprimand. Barely had a month passed by when J.C. was caught again by the CMP, this time for driving an army jeep without an army

'On parade I
like a Scotch
and soda,
off parade I
command a
division'

5 Brig. Mohammad Usman was the highest-ranking Indian officer to have died in the Indo-Pak war of
  1947–1948. He became the symbol of India's secular credentials when at the time of Partition, along
  with many other Muslim officers, he opted to remain in India and declined to move to Pakistan.
6 The GOC's residence.
7 Army's motorcycle rider.

licence. Since this was a second violation within a short span of time, he was marched up to the GOC, escorted by his CO and brigade commander. One look at him and Sam said, 'Sweetie, you are doing extremely well. With three months of service you have come calling on your GOC escorted by two senior officers!' The outcome was a far cry from what J.C. had expected. Sam extolled J.C.'s commonsense initiative and in 26 Infantry Division the rules allowing officers to drive army vehicles were rationalised.

It was during his tenure in Jammu that Sam had his first run-in with Defence Minister Krishna Menon. Menon was a left-wing politician, ambitious and sardonic. He was on an official visit to 26 Infantry Division and casually asked Sam what he thought of Gen. Thimayya, the army chief, with whom he had differences. Thimayya was a brilliant officer, professionally competent and morally upright, whom Sam held in high regard. He replied, 'Mr Minister, I am not allowed to think about him. He is my Chief. Tomorrow you will be asking my brigadiers and colonels what they think of me. It's the surest way to ruin the discipline of the army. Don't do it in the future.' Menon flew into a rage and told Sam to abandon his 'British ways of thinking'. 'I can get rid of Thimayya if I want to!' he thundered. Undeterred, Sam continued that he could, it was his prerogative to do as he wished since he was the defence minister, but that would not deter his resolve not to comment on the next appointee. Menon said nothing at the time but he nursed a grudge that would snowball over the years.

It was not long before Sam and Menon locked horns again. To Sam it was unacceptable that because of a chronic shortage of accommodation, officers returning from field assignments to peace stations should have to wait for months before they were allotted government housing.

*It was during his tenure in Jammu that Sam had his first run-in with Defence Minister Krishna Menon*

This reduced time spent with families before they were deployed again. On taking over 26 Infantry Division his first priority was to speed up the construction of married accommodation.

When the project got underway, the defence minister passed orders that soldiers should be used as construction labour. Sam refused, saying that in his division soldiers would train to fight the enemy, and not be employed as cheap labour. The Military Engineering Service had always been and should continue to be used for this purpose. For a second time Sam's resolve prevailed and Menon had to eat humble pie.

Stories of Gen. Manekshaw sparring with the defence minister spread like wildfire in the army. When the welfare of his men was at stake Sam was ready to take on anyone who stood in the way. It was these qualities that endeared him to rank and file in the army but made him the proverbial thorn in the side of bureaucrats and politicians. By speaking up and holding his ground Sam had qualified his own test of moral courage as 'the ability to distinguish between right and wrong, and having so distinguished, to be prepared to speak up, irrespective of the views held by your superiors or subordinates and the consequences to yourself.' ◆

LEFT TO RIGHT:
**Sam at a Welfare Centre**
Courtesy: 58 Gorkha Training Centre

**As GOC 26 Infantry Division, at site for accommodation for troops**
Courtesy: The Manekshaw family

**As GOC 26 Infantry Division, accompanying General Thimayya on an inspection of barracks**
Courtesy: 58 Gorkha Training Centre

His companion and best
friend, Piffer

**FACING PAGE:**
Farewell from DSSC
Courtesy: 58 Gorkha Training Centre

# Defence Services Staff College and 4 Corps

In 1959 Sam was posted to Wellington as commandant of the Defence Services Staff College. His strategic vision, his extensive professional knowledge and his clear articulation made him an ideal choice. His students remember his brilliant summing up of map exercises, sand model[1] discussions and telephone battles with an unfailing sense of humour. But this tenure would be remembered as much for its high tide of achievement as for its low ebb of victimisation. Defence Minister Krishna Menon, smarting from the snubs Sam had delivered when he was GOC 26 Infantry Division, was biding his time to strike back. Menon had ingratiated himself with Prime Minister Nehru by promoting Lt Gen. B.M. 'Bijji' Kaul, a Kashmiri officer and Nehru's protégé, as Chief of General Staff (CGS)[2] at Army Headquarters. CGS was a powerful appointment in itself but Kaul continued to wrest power and slowly but surely marginalised the army chief, Gen.

---

1 A sand model is the exact replica of terrain of the battle zone with all the geographical and physical features incorporated. Battle plans, prepared by opposing sides, are 'gamed' on a sand model to identify weaknesses.
2 This appointment has since been abolished.

P.N. Thapar (Punjab Regiment). The army chief is always from a fighting arm. Bijji Kaul belonged to the Army Service Corps (ASC), a non-fighting arm. Although he had no combat experience he aspired to become the army chief by eliminating all those who posed a threat to his ambition. When Sam was GOC 26 Infantry Division, Kaul was GOC 4 Infantry Division. Since both divisions were under 15 Corps, during a sand model exercise they were pitted against each other. Kaul was designated 'enemy commander' and Sam was the 'attacking division commander'. The narrative of the exercise portrayed the enemy commander as belonging to a non-fighting arm, professionally inept and deploying his troops to build accommodation at the expense of training. The description fitted Kaul perfectly and he was not too pleased with this characterisation. Sam as the attacking divisional commander dominated the exercise and routed the 'enemy'. At a dinner that followed, Kaul, smarting from defeat and seething with anger, pointed his baton at the slight bulge in Sam's stomach and within earshot of junior officers joked, 'What have you got there?' 'Guts,' said Sam, and the officers had a good laugh. Kaul was left with a shattered ego.

Menon and Kaul colluded to launch a smear campaign to sully Sam's reputation. Menon alleged that Maj. Gen. Sam Manekshaw was too pro-western in his outlook and mannerisms and, therefore, by implication, anti-Indian. His restoration and display of the portraits of eminent British officers like Robert Clive and Warren Hastings in his office, was hyped to condemn him as an unashamed Anglophile. He was alleged to have made a brash statement that he would have no DS at the Staff College whose wife looked like an 'ayah'.[3] After a number of such frivolous charges had been brought against him and the canard spread and repeated, Kaul went for the jugular and initiated a court of inquiry against the commandant. Instructors were approached to provide evidence against Sam. A few officers succumbed to inducements and provided specious evidence but the majority stood by their commandant. It was an acrimonious and unpleasant affair that dragged on for over a year. Outwardly Sam maintained his composure, but it wasn't an easy time. Lt Gen. A.M. 'Vir' Vohra, who was a DS at the Staff College recalls Sam confiding in him that the army was the only institution that he cared for. It was so much a part of his core being that while driving, if he saw a geographical feature, his military mind would immediately plot the best way to defend or attack it. The thought of being sent home at the age of forty-eight was demoralising. Luckily for Sam, Lt Gen. Daulat Singh, GOC-in-C Western Command, the presiding officer of the court of inquiry, was a man of integrity. He is believed to have given some of the witnesses a hard time, asking one, a cavalry officer, how he thought that the Staff College was in any way more western in its outlook than his cavalry regiment. Another witness was told that any honourable officer whose evidence was so devoid of substance should shoot himself in shame! Sam came out unscathed, exonerated of all charges. In spite of this Krishna Menon was unrelenting and hoped to get Sam dismissed from the army. He drafted a letter expressing his severe displeasure with the commandant and directed Army Headquarters to put it on Sam's official service record. A copy of this letter was sent to Sam. 'Beroze,' he said to me, 'if you ever work in MS Branch, look up my dossier. You will see my response and what I told Menon to do with his letter!'

FACING PAGE:
**In a trench with a soldier**
Courtesy: 58 Gorkha Training Centre

3 A native maidservant employed by the British. The term continues to be used commonly for house-
maids even today.

Soon thereafter, nemesis caught up with Menon and Kaul in what is alluded to by military historians as the 'Great Himalayan Blunder'. After his tenure as CGS, Kaul was posted to Tezpur, in NEFA, to command 4 Corps. In October 1962 the Chinese broke through our defences and captured vast tracts of Indian territory. Our soldiers were left facing an overpowering enemy with obsolete weapons and equipment. They were fighting at heights of 15,000 feet without winter clothing, in canvas shoes.[4] Logistical support was non-existent since there were no roads to maintain the supply chain. Forward posts had to be maintained by airdrops that went awry as troops retreated and their ground positions could not be located because of poor communications. Within a short time the Corps was in total disarray. Soldiers succumbed to the adverse effects of high altitude because of rapid deployment without adequate acclimatisation. After taking a large number of prisoners, China declared a ceasefire. With the smoking gun pointing at the corps commander, the chickens finally came home to roost. Kaul was relieved of his command for lack of leadership, tactical acumen and strategic vision. The army chief, Gen. Thapar, submitted his resignation and Menon was sacked.

Sam had been cleared to become a lieutenant general but his promotion had been held in abeyance for eighteen months pending the outcome of the court of inquiry. Officers junior to him had picked up their rank. Sam went to Delhi and sought an interview with Prime Minister Nehru. 'General,' replied a dejected Nehru, 'what can I tell you about your future when I can barely predict my own.' Nehru realised a bit too late that he had been naïve in his assessment of the Chinese. On November 19, 1962 Gen. J.N. 'Muchu' Chaudhuri was appointed as the Chief of the Army Staff (COAS) and on December 2 Sam was promoted to lieutenant general and asked to take over 4 Corps from Kaul. 'It was the Chinese who came to my rescue,' he quipped.

What Sam inherited from Kaul was a demoralised force. His first address to his staff officers had the Manekshaw stamp of brevity and flamboyance, 'Gentlemen, I have arrived. There will

*Sam: '... Remember, we are all expendable; the reputation of the army is not, nor is the honour of the country'*

---

4 B.G. Verghese in the *Times of India*, October 25, 2012.

be no more withdrawals in 4 Corps. Thank you.' His 'Order of the Day' to the Corps was equally cogent, 'From now onwards there will be no withdrawals except on my personal orders which will not be given. We shall stand and fight where we dig in. Remember, we are all expendable; the reputation of the army is not, nor is the honour of the country.' Sam set about, pulling chestnuts out of the fire. Operational plans were revised, forward defences re-sited and strengthened, artillery guns redeployed, ammunition and logistical dumps created, field medical hospitals established, intelligence collection plans refined and procedures for close air support revised.

After the Chinese invasion, the border with China had become a political hot potato and a security issue. Prime Minister Nehru accompanied by Defence Minister Y.B. Chavan, government officials and his daughter, Indira Gandhi, who held no office at the time, decided to visit 4 Corps. While leading the visitors to the Ops Room[5], Sam refused entry to Indira Gandhi, saying, 'Madam, I'm sorry you cannot enter the map room since you have not taken the oath of secrecy.' Indira was not too happy to be excluded, but luckily this episode did not sour their relations. At the briefing Sam impressed everyone with his smart and alert manner, and the confidence he exuded so impressed Chavan that he is believed to have told Nehru to watch this officer for he seemed destined to become chief one day.

As corps commander Sam worked to ensure that the tensions ratcheted up by his predecessor gradually dissipated. His interactions with officers were relaxed but businesslike, confident and resolute. He frequently visited forward areas and displayed a keen eye for the ground.

Welfare was his top priority. Sam struck a deal with the railways to increase the number of seats reserved on trains for army personnel. He liaised with the air force to allow soldiers and officers proceeding on leave to avail of the bi-weekly courier service to Delhi. Sam never broke stride, and within a year 4 Corps was well on its way to making its defences impregnable. ◆

LEFT TO RIGHT:
Dr Radhakrishnan, President of India, visits 4 Corps

In 4 Corps, from left to right, Lieutenant General P.P. Kumaramangalam, Brigadier Jimmy Nadirshaw, Sam and his ADC, Captain P.S. Kalkat

On a more serious note, there are operational plans to discuss. Lieuenant Colonel A.M. (Vir) Vohra, his GSO1 Ops is to his left
Courtesy: 58 Gorkha Training Centre

---

5 Operation Room is where operational plans are discussed.

At Se La with Major
General Onkar Singh
Kalkat, GOC 5 Mountain
Division

**FACING PAGE:**
Tea with the troops in a
forward area
Courtesy: 58 Gorkha Training Centre

# The Army Commander

On December 4, 1963 Sam was posted as General Officer Commanding-in-Chief (GOC-in-C) Western Command, headquartered at Simla. While this tenure was short and uneventful, an incident occurred that raised a great many hackles in political circles. In the summer of 1964, Prime Minister Nehru was critically ill. The Chinese debacle of 1962 had deeply impacted his psyche and he never quite recovered from the humiliation of defeat. Anticipating riots that the PM's death could trigger, the army chief, Gen. 'Muchu' Chaudhuri, ordered a brigade to be moved from Meerut[1] to Delhi for Internal Security (IS) duties. Alarmed at the move, the government concluded that the chief and army commander were planning a coup. While Muchu was able to convince the government that he harboured no ulterior motives, doubts about his and Sam's intentions lingered for many years. Within a year Sam was posted to

1 A city in the neighbouring state of Uttar Pradesh, sixty-eight kilometres from Delhi.

**With officers of 2/8 GR in their Mess in Fort William, Calcutta**

Courtesy: Authors

Calcutta as GOC-in-C Eastern Command. This reinforced the perception that moving troops to Delhi had tainted him with the brush of culpability and the government preferred to put a safe distance between him and the capital. Gen. Chaudhuri could have gone the extra mile to correct this misconception about Sam but he blinked, in spite of which Sam remained steadfastly loyal to his old friend. This was a trait he displayed repeatedly in many of his relationships.

Eastern Command posed a multitude of security challenges with China to the north, East Pakistan (now Bangladesh) on the eastern flank, insurgency in Nagaland and the Mizo hills,[2] and political instability in West Bengal. With his military prowess Sam was successful in every operation that he planned and executed during his tenure as eastern army commander. Forward Defended Localities (FDLs) along the Sikkim border and the strategic pass of Nathu-La were fortified, to block ingress by the Chinese. Improved intelligence collection ensured that the army was a step ahead of the Naga insurgents. In 1968, based on intelligence reports, the army surrounded and captured 300 Nagas, along with their leader Mowu Angami, who were returning from China with arms and ammunition. This took the wind out of a decade-long secessionist movement. Sam's approach to insurgency or any home-grown movement was pragmatic. He believed that the army's role had to be limited to establishing a position of ascendency and creating conditions for political dialogue. To achieve this, he ensured that the troops he commanded were seen as a professional force that was alert, took minimal casualties and played fair but could deal firmly with sedition and disruptive elements.

---

2 Which later became the state of Mizoram on February 20, 1987.

In the 1960s a Marxist (communist) movement frequently brought the city of Calcutta down on its knees with calls for 'bandhs' (strikes) and street demonstrations. My battalion, 2/8 GR had followed Sam to Calcutta and was garrisoned at Fort William. Soon after its arrival there was a 'bandh' and the city went into lockdown mode. The local administration clamped a curfew and called out the army. 'A' Company was patrolling the inner precincts of the city when the convoy came to a dead halt. The road ahead had been barricaded with mountains of household furniture. The company commander, Maj. Raghu Thorat, ordered the Gorkhas to alight, load the furniture into the army three-ton trucks, clear the roadblock and continue. The agitators were stumped. Their intimidation tactics would no longer be countenanced and moreover their furniture had been confiscated. The next day 'A' Company patrolled the same route, unhampered. There were no barricades. In fact, at the very sight of a Gorkha 'Johnny' the aspiring communists took to their heels with cries of 'Gorkha eshechhe' (the Gorkhas have arrived). For a long time thereafter, at Sam's recommendation,

a Gorkha battalion was stationed at Fort William. After years of concerted effort, the movement eventually lost momentum.

From April 1965 the frequency and intensity of border skirmishes between India and Pakistan on the western front increased and by August the storms of war were gathering momentum. The army was placed on high alert. With characteristic foresight Sam advised the army chief that the offensive should be limited to the western front and a holding operation considered in the east so as not to antagonise the East Pakistanis. In his reckoning, India had nothing to gain by expanding the conflict. Gen. Chaudhuri

*Sam's strategy paid rich dividends in 1971 when East Pakistanis saw the Indian Army as saviours rather than aggressors*

At 2/8 GR Raising Day celebration. Seated on the sofa (right), from left to right, are Mrs Vijay Sisodia, Sam, Mrs Dewan and Sherry
Courtesy: 2/8 Gorkha Rifles

agreed with Sam's assessment. War broke out on September 6 when Pakistan pushed infiltrators into J&K to instigate insurgency. Ground and air strikes were also launched along the entire western border from the Punjab to Gujarat. In the thick of war, Gen. Chaudhuri visited Calcutta for an overnight consultation with Sam in whose military acumen he had immense faith. The conflict raged for sixteen days until ceasefire was declared on September 22. The war had been contained in the western sector. Sam's strategy paid rich dividends in 1971 when East Pakistanis saw the Indian Army as saviours rather than aggressors.

After the war I accompanied Sam, his GSO1 (Ops)[3] and GSO1 (Int)[4] on a goodwill visit to Dacca (now Dhaka). Maj. Gen. Fazal Muqeem Khan, GOC 12 Infantry Division, received the eastern army commander with a great deal of warmth. Prior to Independence they had both

---

3 Operations.
4 Intelligence.

*After Ferozepur and Jammu this [Calcutta] was the third time the battalion was stationed with him and his closeness to the officers and the soldiers grew*

served in the 4/12 FFR. Putting his arm around Fazal's shoulders Sam said, *'Chalo ghar, begum ko milne jate hai.'* (Let's go home to meet the lady of the house.) With that they disappeared, leaving business to be sorted out by their respective staff officers.

With 2/8 GR posted in Calcutta the army commander was a frequent guest at battalion functions: *bara khanas,*[5] sports events, Dussehra[6] celebrations, Raising Day, battle honour days[7] and mess nights.[8] After Ferozepur and Jammu this was the third time the battalion was stationed with him and his closeness to the officers and the soldiers grew.

In 1967 'Muchu' Chaudhuri retired and Gen. P.P. Kumaramangalam, popularly known as 'K', took over as army chief. In September that year, we were in Delhi for a month. Sam was officiating army chief, when there was a serious skirmish with the Chinese on the Sikkim border that lasted two weeks and saw a heavy exchange of artillery fire. None of his senior staff was with him so I was required to brief him each morning. He wanted details on the progress of battle, the number of artillery rounds fired, casualty count on our side, casualties inflicted on the enemy, status of reinforcements, and operational strategy. I would call Lt Gen. Jagjit Singh Aurora, GOC 33 Corps and Maj. Gen. Sagat Singh, GOC 17 Mountain Division at 6.00 am and have my brief ready before

---

5 *Bara khana* literally translates as 'the big meal' when the entire battalion gathers on an open ground for
  a lavish feast attended by soldiers, JCOs, officers and in some regiments by the wives and children.
6 An important Hindu festival celebrating the victory of good over evil. It is the most important festival
  for Gorkhas and celebrated for an entire week by the Gorkha regiments.
7 Battle honour days commemorate hard fought battle victories.
8 Mess nights are formal dinners in the mess where attendance by officers is mandatory and regimental
  traditions and protocols are strictly observed.

**Inspecting a ceremonial parade on the occasion of 2/8 GR Raising Day**
Courtesy: 2/8 Gorkha Rifles

breakfast. Although both sides took casualties, the intruders were repulsed with bloodied noses. The Chinese lost 400 men, most of their bunkers were razed to the ground and they were unable to get a foothold on our FDLs. It was a very different Indian Army from the one they had overrun in 1962.

In spite of this volatile situation on many fronts, Sam's posting in Calcutta was one of the best of his career. His official car was a silver grey Austin Sheerline 125 A of 1940 vintage. This stately guzzler used to be the official car of Gen. Sir Roy Bucher when he was C-in-C. With his departure it had been garaged at Army HQ Transport Company in Delhi. As DMO, Sam had his eye on this car and Gen. Bucher had jested that try as he might, he could never hope to have an Austin Sheerline as his official car. The comment had never ceased to rankle and when he became eastern army commander he had the jalopy retrieved and brought to Calcutta. Work on the engine, a silver coat of paint and new leather upholstery restored it to its pristine glory. Sam had become a respected figure in the city to which he had brought a modicum of sanity. In spite of the chaotic traffic, the police and the public alike recognised the army commander's car and made way for the 'silver queen' as it wound its way through the streets of Calcutta.

Arriving in Delhi to officiate as COAS. Behind Sam is the author, his ADC

**BELOW:**
The Austin Sheerline
Courtesy: Authors

The army commander followed a strict routine. Each morning his driver, Havildar[9] Krishna, would pick me up from my room at 8.00 am and drive me to Command House in Alipore. After a short briefing from his JCO ADC, Subedar Maj. Lal Bahadur Pun (6/8 GR), I would join the family for breakfast, a meal Sam believed no soldier should ever skip. I was often treated to a Parsi savoury that Silloo would have saved for me, or some exotic delicacy that the army commander had tried his hand at. Breakfast over, the Austin would pull up in the porch and as soon as the doors were opened Sam's dogs, Piffer, named after his old regiment 4/12 FFR, Caesar and Kalo, would jump in and make themselves comfortable, leaving the army commander and me to find our places as best as we could. On reaching the office, the canine brigade would be the first to alight and head straight for the air-conditioned comfort of the office where they would lounge and slumber, unperturbed by comings and goings, till noon, when Lal Bahadur Saab, returning from his round of chores, would come by the office and take them back to Command House.

The first order of the day was the 9.00 am briefing by his GSO1 (Ops) and GSO1 (Int) followed by similar briefings by the heads of all arms and services. Important developments within the command were reported and discussed. Sam expected his staff officers, regardless of rank, to participate

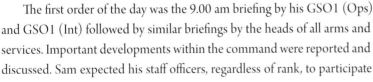

9 A havildar is a senior non-commissioned officer.

At Calcutta airport
receiving Prime Minister
Lal Bahadur Shastri
Courtesy: 58 Gorkha Training Centre

and speak their minds during these discussions. After hearing them out, he would sum up, 'Okay chaps, I've heard your views. Now, this is what we will do.' Work would be delegated and the day would begin. On Sundays, holidays and when we were on tours the responsibility to brief him fell to my lot. 'So Beroze, how's my Command doing?' would be his first question. In 1967 we were on an official tour to Panagarh (West Bengal). I called Command Headquarters, Calcutta for the SITREP[10] on an operation underway in the Mizo hills, took copious notes and gave a detailed briefing down to platoon level. Sam patted my back and said, 'Good job, Beroze, one day you *might* make a good staff officer!' My duties as an aide were not limited to mere logistics. As a young captain I was given the same insight into every level of function and decision-making as was Sam's senior staff. I was required to read all his correspondence and be aware of his comments and decisions. This meant access to sensitive material and required the highest level of confidentiality. It was the trust that Sam reposed in his staff that brought out the best in them.

Sam's style of command was informal. He would walk into the rooms of his staff officers for consultations. Short-circuiting military protocol, he would pick up the phone and speak directly

10 Situation Report.

to a commanding officer in a forward area, 'Sweetie, this is your army commander speaking.' Initially, this unnerved many junior officers, but soon it became established practice. Word also got out that while Sam broke all barriers of formality he was not to be trifled with. Those who quibbled or lied soon found to their dismay that Sam was unforgiving and ruthless in dealing with dishonesty or deception. He had the memory of an elephant and without a scrap of paper in front of him he could repeat verbatim what had been said to him, months earlier.

As ADC it was my responsibility to organise the army commander's tours. Sam had a set regimen to visit all formations in his command by rotation but those located in inhospitable, snow-bound regions and formations engaged in active counter-insurgency operations were visited more frequently. He preferred to size up the situation personally, review operational plans periodically and ensure that logistical support and the safety of the troops would not be compromised under any circumstances.

During tours he would reach out to soldiers on the front lines. Throwing all arrangements out of gear he would ask for puri and sabzi[11] from the *langar*[12] and share a mug of brewed 'chai' (tea) with the boys, skipping breakfast at the Officers' Mess. He seized every opportunity to mingle with the troops, check their living conditions, the quality of their meals and address their concerns. Woe betide the CO and subedar major who were indifferent to the welfare of the soldier.

Sam cared equally for his officers. On tours, he would carry the latest LP[13] records, chocolates and sometimes a stack of Playboy magazines or Playboy calendars. All these gifts were paid for from his personal account.

There were those special tours that we all looked forward to. Picturesque Sikkim[14] was a hot favourite, a tour that Silloo never missed. As an army commander's wife she was entitled to accompany her husband within his command. The *Chogyal*,[15] an honorary colonel of the 8th Gorkha Rifles, insisted that we stay at his luxurious palace. We would take an Indian Airlines flight to Bagdogra from where an IAF Alouette helicopter would take us directly to the palace grounds in Gangtok. Early morning we would set off by jeep, driving through steep mountain roads to visit units in their FDLs and return late in the evening.

Dinner at the palace would be a long-drawn-out affair that would carry on well past midnight. A few hours of sleep and the next morning we'd be headed to another FDL. This routine would be repeated for the duration of our stay until

*He would pick up the phone and speak directly to a commanding officer in a forward area, 'Sweetie, this is your army commander speaking'*

**Sam's dogs with his Gorkhas**
Courtesy: The Manekshaw family

---

11 Fried flat bread and vegetable.
12 Soldiers' kitchen.
13 Long playing records that were popular in the 1960s.
14 At the time Sikkim was an independent country and merged with India only in May 1975 as a result of a referendum conducted to abolish the monarchy.
15 The title given to the monarch of Sikkim.

*... the Mizo problem commandeered Sam's attention throughout his tenure as army commander*

Addressing officers at HQ Eastern Command, Calcutta
Courtesy: Authors

FACING PAGE:
In the garden with granddaughter, Brandy
Courtesy: The Manekshaw family

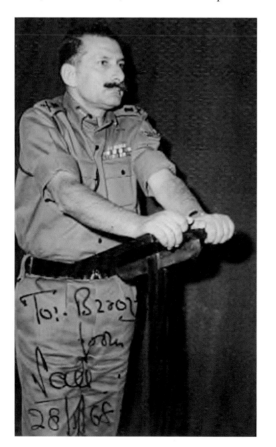

Sam was satisfied that he had covered all the ground he planned to. Equally enchanting was the kingdom of Bhutan except that Sam being an avid angler, the day began with trout fishing at 4.00 am! The army commander kept a punishing schedule. His stamina, his energy and his eye for detail ensured that his staff was always on their toes.

Not all tours were as enchanting. I recall one in particular to the Mizo hills. On February 28, 1966 Pu Laldenga, leader of the Mizo National Front (MNF), demanded independence from India. The army commander was dining at the 2/8 GR Officers' Mess when he received a phone call that the MNF had formally launched a secessionist movement and the army had been ordered to crack down. The next day, accompanied by the GSO1 (Ops), Lt Col. 'Freddie' Freemantle, we flew to Kumbhigram airbase at Masimpur. On landing we were informed that the insurgents had captured a water point that was the only source of drinking water for the 1st Assam Rifles post at Lungleh. Brig. Rusi Kabraji (Corps of Signals), commander, 61 Infantry Brigade, under whom the Mizo hills sector came, began his briefing and presented his plan. Being a Parsi he peppered his presentation with the choicest Gujarati[16] swear words. With an expressionless face Sam listened patiently for five minutes till he could take it no more, 'Rusi, I am impressed with your eloquence and your vocabulary. Now, can I have your operational plans!' The briefing was completed sans embellishments. While we were at the base an IAF Caribou was preparing to carry out a sortie and drop water at the Lungleh post. Sam decided on the spur of the moment to take a lift on the aircraft and assess the situation first hand from the air. Freddie and I accompanied him. The pilot circled the post to select a vantage point for the drop. As he began to descend we came under heavy small-arms fire. The port-side engine took a direct hit and was rendered out of action. The pilot had no choice but to abort the sortie, gain height and head back to Kumbhigram on one engine. Bullets continued to fly and pierce the aircraft till we were out of range. IAF fighter aircraft were scrambled to escort us to base. Through all of this the army commander remained calm and unperturbed, discussing plans with his GSO1 (Ops). On landing we counted sixteen bullet holes. Counter insurgency operations were launched but the Mizo problem commandeered Sam's attention throughout this tenure. It was finally resolved only after the state of Mizoram was created in 1987.

As army commander, Sam's role was not limited to the eastern sector. He was invited to visit military training establishments that laid a high value on his vision and his insight.

On most tours Sam's orderly would sit next to him on the aircraft. On one occasion, we were returning from Bagdogra and I needed to brief him, so I displaced the 'Johnny'. Briefing over, like a true soldier, I fell

---

16 Gujarati is the mother tongue of the Parsis.

At an FDL
Courtesy: 58 Gorkha Training Centre

asleep and woke up only when the army commander prodded me. 'Get up you damn chap, we've reached Calcutta!' My head had been resting on his arm throughout the flight and he had sat motionless so as not to disturb me. I opened my eyes to be told off some more, 'Beroze, sometimes you act like I am your ADC!'

In spite of Eastern Command being operationally committed, army life in the 1960s was comparatively easy-going. At times we would be done with the business of the day by noon. Sam would call for his staff car and we would drive to Park Street. He would purchase the latest LPs either to augment his collection or as gifts for the officers' mess on a forthcoming tour. Every other week we would visit Ennis, a hair salon. Sam was very particular about his grooming. If I happened to accompany him, I was treated to a 'decent haircut'. The barber would be done with his hair in short order, while my hair being much thicker, took longer to cut. Sam would be waiting for me in the reception, feigning impatience. On our return to the office he would complain to his staff about how he had been suckered by his ADC to pay for his haircut and, to add insult to injury, he had to wait while 'the damn chap' wallowed in luxury and got a head and neck massage! Sam loved to indulge his staff but he also loved to embellish the narrative and make it seem like he was being taken for a right royal ride.

At the end of the year I earned my first report from the army commander. It simply said, 'This officer is a Parsi but has all the attributes of a Gorkha. He is bound to get into trouble one day.'

Calcutta was a vibrant city in the 1960s in spite of the disruptive tactics of the communists. Park Street, the downtown area, was a stone's throw from Fort William. Restaurants offered good cuisine, live music and great nightlife. With all these attractions Calcutta did not sit easy on the

**Fishing in Bhutan**
Courtesy: 58 Gorkha Training Centre

wallet of a young officer. Sam was a dapper army commander, immaculately turned out for each occasion. He had a fad that his ADC should dress exactly like him. This did not present a challenge for army functions where I had to be in uniform, but to keep up with his civilian wardrobe from Marks and Spencer and his Savile Row suits was beyond the means of a lieutenant who made Rs 400 a month. I possessed just one suit, outfitted at the IMA, which was far from sufficient for the varied social commitments in Calcutta. I wore it for all occasions that demanded formal civilian attire. A few months after my arrival, I received a dressing down. Sam told me that when he wore tweeds he expected me to do likewise and if he wore a combination, blazer and flannels, so should I. I replied that the Government of India did not pay me adequately to live up to his expectations. He turned in a huff and strode out of my office. Both of us sulked for a few hours and the episode was laid to rest, or so I thought. A week later, on completion of the day's work, Sam asked for his car. The Austin Sheerline arrived and Havildar Krishna was asked to drive to the Bombay Dyeing showroom on Park Street. I helped the army commander select material for a blazer and a tweed jacket. He settled the bill and we returned to Command House for lunch. As I stepped out of the car Sam handed me the packet and said, 'Here, Beroze, get yourself two decent jackets.' I thanked him for the gift, but got under his skin for a second time, asking how he expected me to pay the tailoring charges! He muttered something about me being a damn ungrateful chap and taking advantage of his kindness, but the tailor had been summoned to Command House and was waiting to take my measurements. The jackets were delivered and Sam insisted on paying for them although my comment had been in a lighter vein. I had grown very close to him and enjoyed the thrust and parry of our conversations as much as he did. While I did venture to take a

*Sam was a dapper army commander ... He had a fad that his ADC should dress exactly like him*

Presenting a trophy to
a 2/8 GR soldier while
the commanding officer,
Lieutenant Colonel R.S.
Pathania, looks on

Courtesy: 2/8 Gorkha Rifles

*While I did venture to take a few liberties with him [Sam], I knew where to draw the line*

few liberties with him, I knew where to draw the line. This practice of stocking my wardrobe continued ever after, even after I stopped working for him. Every now and again Sam would bring me a suit from England as a gift. I have ensured that I still fit into most of them since I value the memories they bring back of the good old days.

On Saturdays the Race Course was a popular watering hole for officers posted in Calcutta and their wives. The army commander had a special box. Through Zavare Wadia, steward of the course, Sam had arranged for all service officers to be granted access to the prestigious Members' Lawn for a nominal fee of Rs 5, the only requirement being that they had to be formally attired. Race mania would consume Command Headquarters on Saturday mornings. Officers would pour over the *Cole*,[17] the local punting guide, and discuss betting options, but all their research would come to naught for at the crack of the gun the horses would take to their heels but often in the wrong direction, heading straight back to their stables! As a routine, on Saturdays I was invited to lunch by Sherry and her husband, Dinky, after which I would accompany them to the races. The first time round my voracious appetite delayed their arrival at the Race Course. Sam was annoyed at their tardiness. When Sherry was asked what had caused the delay she simply pointed at me and said, 'Father, don't ask me, ask your ADC, he wouldn't stop eating.' Thereafter, every Saturday at 10.00 am Sam would order me out of the office, 'Go on, Beroze, off you go! Start eating your lunch *now* and make sure you don't delay my daughter!'

Sam was a stickler for military precision and punctuality. For all official engagements I would coordinate his arrival and departure down to the wire. If we were running early, Krishna would be made to slow down to arrive on the dot. It was the same with departure; I would give Sam the heads-up, 'Last drink, Sir, we must leave in fifteen minutes.' An enthusiastic host who plied him with 'one for the road' often found to his chagrin that the general would hand me the drink, 'Here, Beroze, make sure this is not wasted.' I had to gulp it down, bottoms up! The problem was that I drank rum while the general drank Scotch. In the bargain I learned to mix my drinks and hold them well. If his stomach was lined with steel so was mine.

In spite of this precision planning 'snafus'[18] happened and when they did Sam never lost his cool. We returned to Calcutta from a tour to find that his staff car was not on the tarmac as per

---

17 The *Cole* is a guide for race-goers. It contains every bit of information related to a race: the number of horses, their lineage, weight, owners, trainers, jockeys, previous record and current morning workout forms besides the betting tips.
18 An acronym used frequently in the army, standing for 'situation normal, all fouled up'.

standard practice. It was held up somewhere in a traffic snarl. The station wagon, meant for his luggage, had made it to the airport. Without a fuss, Sam got into the vehicle tucked between his bags, minus his star plate and flag, and told the driver, Shivaji, to take him home.

The Manekshaws' personal car was a Sunbeam Rapier, mostly used by Silloo. One Sunday Sam decided to drive himself to the office in the Sunbeam. He was dressed casually in his weekend outfit, shorts and Peshawari sandals.[19] At the entrance to Fort William he was stopped by the Gorkha sentry and asked to present his identity card. Sam had left the card at home and was denied entry. Out of curiosity Sam asked the 'Johnny', *'Malai chine chaina? Ma tero army commander choon.'* (Don't you recognise me? I'm your army commander.) The Gorkha who was probably a rookie gave an honest response, *'Na, chinaey chaina. ID chaina, pheta chaina, jhanda chaina, gari ma star plate chaina. Kasri chinne ho ki tapai army commander cha.'* (No, I don't recognise you. You don't have an identity card, you have no badges of rank, your car has no flag and no star plate. How am I expected to believe you are the army commander?) Sam asked the Gorkha if he could make a call from the sentry booth. Permission was luckily granted. Speaking to the commanding officer he said, 'Pat, one of your boys has stopped me at the gate. Not his fault, I am out of uniform, without my ID and driving my private car. Can you bail me out?' The CO was there in a flash. Sam was identified and allowed to enter Fort William and the 'Johnny' Gorkha got a pat on his shoulder for perfect sentry duty.

---

19 Sandals worn in Peshawar (now Pakistan) by the local Pashtuns were a hot favourite with British Army officers and continue to be worn in South Asia by men in the summers.

**Sand model briefing at the College of Military Engineering (CME), Pune**
Courtesy: 58 Gorkha Training Centre

*In 1968 Sam
was awarded
the Padma
Bhushan for
his astute
handling of
the Mizo hills
insurrection*

It was during Sam's tenure as army commander that Calcutta acquired multi-storeyed residential buildings for officers. Turning down a suggestion to call it 'Manekshaw Complex' he settled for 'Turf View' since the flats had a commanding view of the Race Course. A spanking new Eastern Command Officers' Mess was constructed and plans were afoot for a modern, well-equipped hospital in New Alipore. After he became chief, Sam was invited to Calcutta to lay the foundation stone of the new Command Hospital.

In 1968 Sam was awarded the Padma Bhushan[20] for his astute handling of the Mizo hills insurrection. For the first time a civilian award was given to a military officer. There were no instructions from the adjutant general's (AG's) branch in Delhi as to where this medal should be worn in order of precedence. I was in the dressing room with him, debating where he should pin it. On the spur of the moment we decided that since it was a civilian medal it should be worn below army medals. That impromptu decision set a precedent that became standard protocol in the Indian Army. The government has since changed its policy and the Padma series awards are no longer given to service personnel.

In April 1968, 2/8 GR completed its tenure in Calcutta and moved to 5 Mountain Division, NEFA. In June I decided to revert to the battalion. I had completed three years of staff assignment and needed to clock in regimental service in a field area. My successor was Capt.(later Maj. Gen.) Shubhi Sood of 4/8 GR.

In the 1960s army commanders retired at the age of fifty-four years or after four years of command, whichever was earlier. Sam would have completed four years of command in

**Departing Calcutta to take
over as chief of the army staff**
Courtesy: 58 Gorkha Training Centre

20 The third highest civilian award in India.

Laying the foundation
stone of the Command
Hospital in Calcutta
Courtesy: 58 Gorkha Training Centre

December 1967 and retired, except that 'Muchu' Chaudhuri set great store by his potential. He told the government that there would be no war for the next two years. He suggested that Gen. Kumaramangalam be made the next chief and Sam given a two-year extension. The government agreed and in April 1969 Sam was selected to be chief of the army staff. This announcement was widely celebrated in the army.

Departure from Calcutta evoked mixed feelings. It meant leaving behind his brother Jan and his family. It also meant saying au revoir to the many friends they had made in the city: Zavare Wadia, steward of the Royal Calcutta Turf Club (RCTC); Sir Biren Mookerji, president of the RCTC and chairman of Martin Burns; Cushrow Irani, editor of *The Statesman*, a leading English daily; Dara Antia of Union Carbide; Keshub Mahindra of Mahindra and Mahindra; Dolly Kanga of Calcutta Electric Supply Company; K.C. Maitra, chairman of Guest Keen Williams; Lakshmipat Singhania of the JK Group; secretaries and members of the Tollygunj Club and the Saturday Club and the consul general of the US. Down the road Sam was able to leverage these contacts to facilitate the placement and rehabilitation of retired and wounded army personnel, never for personal gain.

Preparations for the move to Delhi began. Since Sam was very fond of the Austin Sheerline, it was suggested that he take it to Delhi as his official car. He turned down the proposal; he would never allow himself to stoop to that level. On May 29, 1969 Sam took the salute at a farewell ceremony at the Parade Grounds, drove to Dum Dum airport and, with his wife and ADC, boarded an IAF Avro HS 748 bound for Delhi on his last posting. ◆

With JCO ADC, Honorary
Captain Lal Bahadur Pun

FACING PAGE:
Colours of the Grenadiers
Regiment being paraded at
their centre in Nasirabad

Courtesy: 58 Gorkha Training Centre

# The 'Jangi Lat'— Chief of Army Staff

On June 7, 1969 Gen. S.H.F.J. Manekshaw assumed office as India's eighth chief of the army staff. He was the first Indian commissioned officer to be appointed chief. His 'Special Order of the Day' to the army was the shortest ever, 'I have today taken over as Chief of Army Staff, I expect everyone to do his duty.'

Prime Minister Indira Gandhi signed off on Sam's appointment as COAS, but the political lobby close to her continued to question his motive in moving the troops from Meerut to Delhi when he was the western army commander. They feared that Sam's appeal, not just within the army but within the armed forces, combined with his popularity on main street, made him the most likely general to pull off a successful coup. Soon after he had taken over as chief, Mrs Gandhi, whose political capital was not at its peak, decided to clear the air. She invited him for a cup of tea to her office in Parliament House, where he found her quite distressed and emotional. When he learnt that he was the cause of her anxiety, with impeccable chivalry he offered his shoulder for her to cry on. 'Everyone says you are going to take over from me,' she said. 'And do you think I will?' he asked. 'You can't,' she replied. 'Why? Do you think I am so incompetent?' In his most charming manner he was able to reassure her that he harboured no political ambitions whatsoever. A coup spelt disaster for the country and the army, he would never entertain the thought. With an assurance that he would not pull the rug from under her feet, the stage was set for an excellent working relationship.

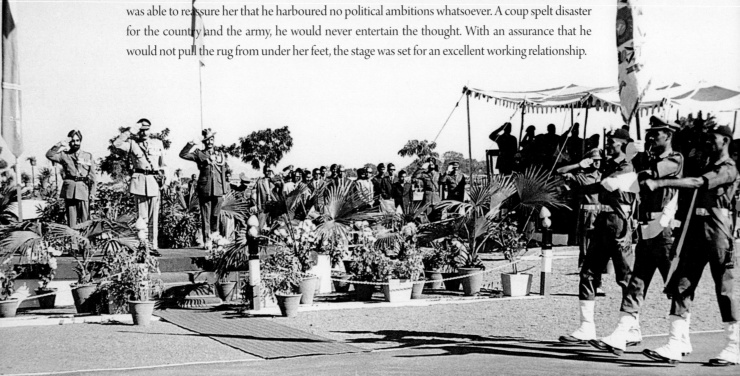

As COAS Sam was now entitled to two aides. I was attending the 81mm Mortar Course at the Infantry School in Mhow when I received a signal from my battalion. I had been posted as ADC to the chief. I completed the course in July and joined him in Delhi.

As chief Sam kept a very spartan office. The only adornments were a pencil sketch of Mahatma Gandhi and bronze statues of two VCs,[1] Havildar Lachhman Gurung of 4/8 GR and Havildar Agan Singh Rai of 2/5 GR.

His first priority as chief was to ensure that the Indian Army was a formidable force with cutting-edge weapons and technology at its command. Additional armoured brigades were raised to meet operational requirements. The production of the indigenous Vijayanta tank was speeded up. Shortages of military hardware such as trawl tanks used to clear anti-tank mines, bridge-laying tanks and armoured recovery vehicles were made good through imports. To match the mobility of armour, selected infantry battalions were mechanised. Artillery regiments were equipped with long-range guns and enhanced mobility. Training establishments were modernised and reorganised and their syllabi, that had earlier focused on lessons learnt from WWII, were replaced by analysis of wars fought by independent India and geared towards future flashpoints of conflict on the subcontinent. Keenly aware of financial constraints, modernisation was balanced with cost-effectiveness. Training for armoured and mechanised regiments on

**Bidding farewell to General P.P. Kumaramangalam at Palam airport, New Delhi**
Courtesy: 58 Gorkha Training Centre

1 Victoria Cross awardees.

'tank simulators', demonstrated during our visit to the USSR, was introduced in the Indian Army, thereby reducing the wear and tear on expensive equipment. No detail was too minor for Sam. When he found out that an Italian fashion designer was in town, staying at the Oberoi Hotel in Delhi, he hired the gentleman to redesign the uniform of the Military Nursing Service (MNS).

Soon after Sam became chief the government was considering the disbandment of 61 Cavalry, the only horse regiment in the Indian Army. Since '61 Cav' had an excellent polo team, it was viewed by the ministry as a 'colonial relic' and marked for 'extinction'. Sam was able to convince the government of the importance of retaining some degree of military pomp and splendour for ceremonial occasions. He won the day and as a mark of gratitude, the officers of 61 Cavalry appointed him colonel of their regiment. This established a precedent and to this day the COAS, by virtue of his appointment, is the Colonel of 61 Cavalry.

The COAS at his desk
Courtesy: Authors

Welfare measures had always been Sam's strongest suit. When his daughter, Maja, informed him that the state of the Armed Forces Clinic (AFC) on Dalhousie Road was a disgrace, he decided to spring a surprise visit. Mid-morning he asked for his staff car and Naik Kani Ram was told to drive us to the AFC. Out of sheer concern I asked if he was not feeling well, only to be rebuked, 'Beroze, do I look like a sick man to you?' Silence reigned supreme thereafter till we reached the clinic. I was told to call the director general of the Armed Forces Medical Services, the adjutant general, the quarter-master general and the engineer-in-chief. 'Tell them to drop everything and come here immediately.' Within a week the blueprint of a new clinic had been drawn, funds were sanctioned and work commenced. In six months the AFC was transformed into a spanking new air-conditioned facility with state-of-the-art equipment. Similarly, when Jeroo, wife of Commodore Dorab Mehta, told him that she did not patronise the CSD[2] canteen at South Block because it was poorly stocked, he visited the canteen unannounced and met the manager to identify impediments and speed up procurement. Within weeks the canteen became an attractive shopping option for service personnel and their families.

Sam was convinced that his officers should have the best facilities for sports and recreation and once these facilities existed, they should be patronised by men in uniform. He set the pace and the Defence Services Officers' Institute (DSOI) at Dhaula Kuan flourished under his patronage. He made it a point to host army functions at the institute rather than at five-star hotels. Diwali melas[3] and flower shows were crowd-pullers. The May Queen Ball, Independence Day Ball and

*Sam was convinced that his officers should have the best facilities for sports and recreation ...*

---

2 Canteen Stores Department of the army.
3 Diwali is the festival of lights. At this time 'melas' or fairs are organised as part of the celebrations.

'I promise to stay out of
your business if you stay
out of mine'
Courtesy: 58 Gorkha Training Centre

*Our cottage
had a small
garden that
Sam took
upon himself
to tend along
with the
much larger
one of Army
House*

New Year's Eve Ball were sold-out events that required advance booking. At these functions, Sam would put in an appearance with Silloo and mingle with members. Silloo was a regular at the Sunday tambola and brunch sessions. The DSOI was transformed into a vibrant club.

On the personal front, settling down in Delhi was no cakewalk. Army House, the chief's residence at 4 King George's Avenue (now Rajaji Marg), needed renovation and, for the first time, Sam was at the mercy of the CPWD[4] which is responsible for the upkeep of ministerial and VIP bungalows in Lutyens' Delhi.[5]

At times like this the services of Maj. Girdhari Lal (Army Service Corps) were requisitioned. Girdhari was an old faithful whose association with Sam went back to pre-independence days when Sam was a captain and the quarter-master of 4/12 FFR and Girdhari was the quarter-master of the 5th Baluch Regiment[6]. Girdhari was a go-getter who had no hesitation in using all the means at his command, including some colourful Punjabi jingoisms, to get a task accomplished. Sam's ardent fan, he had managed to outmanoeuvre the system and trail him on all postings. In dealing with the likes of the CPWD Shubhi and I were considered greenhorns who played by the rules and made no headway. Girdhari on the other hand knew the right balance between wielding the

4 Central Public Works Department.
5 The plush area of Delhi, with ministerial bungalows and gardens, that was designed by Sir Edwin Lutyens.
6 Now with the Pakistan Army.

carrot and stick. He also knew the value of 'universal currency', a bottle of XXX army rum, and the magic it could work. Gradually, Army House began to take shape and was transformed into a home. But one issue continued to defy solution.

Every general has his fads and Sam's was his shower. The water had to be steaming hot and the pressure high, else his day got off to a bad start and the negative effects cascaded to his staff. Try as they might, the CPWD could not fix the problem and the shower at Army House worked in fits and starts. Girdhari was put on the job and without much ado he set his hounds on the CPWD's heels. The shower worked perfectly for a week but lapsed back to spluttering and squirting. Sam's patience was wearing thin, whereupon Girdhari decided that it was time to fall back on the army and call the MES. The Garrison Engineer (GE) struggled with the shower, but to no avail. Weeks turned to months and the COAS was not a happy camper. One evening we returned from work and Sam made a beeline for his bathroom. Girdhari, in uniform and boots, was ordered to get inside the bathtub and Sam turned on the shower. Water spluttered in erratic bursts, evoking loud protests from a drenching Girdhari who swore in choicest Punjabi to wreck havoc on the GE. He asked Sam for one more fortnight to sort the matter out for good. After fifteen days, miraculously, the shower worked without a hiccup, but try as we might, Girdhari refused to divulge how he had wrought this miracle. The story came to light after several months, by which time it had to be accepted, fait accompli. Using Sam's name, Girdhari told MS Branch to post out the incumbent GE who had completed his tenure in Delhi. His replacement was an officer desperate to be stationed in a big city for personal reasons. On arrival in Delhi, the new GE's first port of call was the army chief's bathroom. Girdhari clearly articulated the quid pro quo: the duration of his stay in Delhi hinged entirely on the functioning of the chief's shower. The day the shower malfunctioned he would find himself back in a bunker, facing either China or Pakistan! Needless to say, that was not necessary.

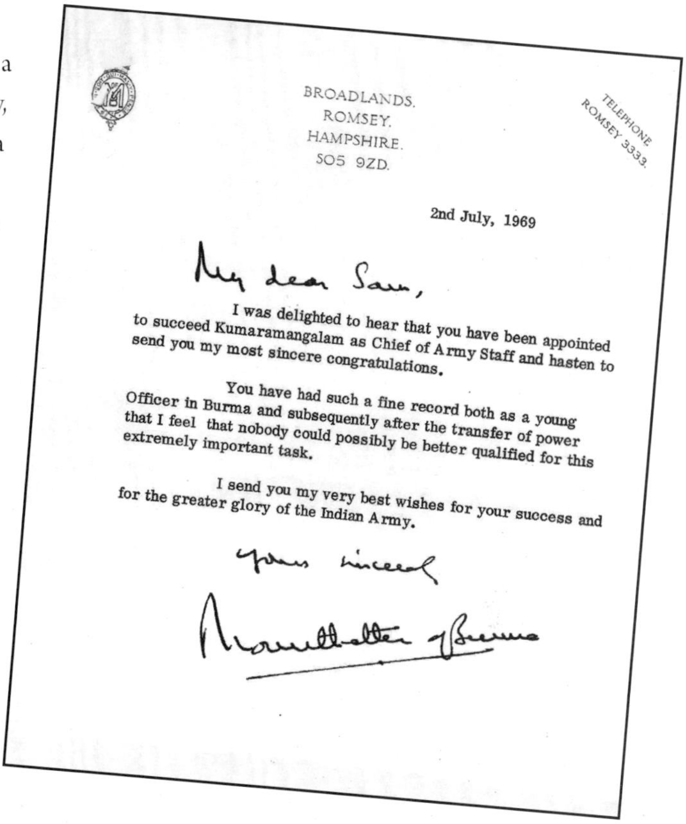

BROADLANDS.
ROMSEY.
HAMPSHIRE.
SO5 9ZD.

TELEPHONE
ROMSEY 3333.

2nd July, 1969

My dear Sam,

I was delighted to hear that you have been appointed to succeed Kumaramangalam as Chief of Army Staff and hasten to send you my most sincere congratulations.

You have had such a fine record both as a young Officer in Burma and subsequently after the transfer of power that I feel that nobody could possibly be better qualified for this extremely important task.

I send you my very best wishes for your success and for the greater glory of the Indian Army.

Yours sincerely

Mountbatten of Burma

**Letter of congratulations from Lord Louis Mountbatten**

Courtesy: The Manekshaw family

Meanwhile, Shubhi and I settled down in our new home, the ADCs' cottage. Accustomed to living in one-room accommodation in a mess, we had no furnishings for a large house. The living and dining rooms were barren except for MES furniture and a few military mementos. We returned from work one evening to find the doors and windows draped with beige and brown silk curtains. Silloo had strolled over to the cottage while we were at work and realised our predicament. With the uncanny knack that army wives possess, she salvaged Sherry's Air India uniform sarees and had them tailored into a set of smart silk curtains that fetched us many compliments. Our cottage had a small garden that Sam took upon himself to tend along with the much larger one of Army House. As a result we had roses, sweet peas, chrysanthemums and perennials that were a luxury for us bachelors. At the crack of dawn, when we were still in bed after a night of partying, the army chief along with the *mali*[7] would be working in our garden! No aides before or after us could possibly have had it this good!

One day while doing the rounds of Army House Sam asked me why all the Gorkhas and all his civilian household staff proudly displayed his picture in their quarters except his aides. My response was that we saw him at work and we saw him at home, we saw him from dawn to dusk; did he really expect us to keep his photograph in our bedrooms too!

Life in Delhi settled into a routine. Each morning began with the pre-departure drill. Accompanied by Shubhi and me, the JCO ADC and Maj. Girdhari Lal, the chief would do a brisk round of the house, giving orders to his staff. At 8.30 am sharp his Chevrolet Impala would pull into the porch with Naik Kani Ram at the wheel and we would leave for Army Headquarters, a five-minute drive from home. To see us off there would be one JCO ADC, two orderlies and four dogs, Piffer, Kalo, Caeser and the newest addition, 'Maatches',[8] a stray, picked up by Maja and christened by the Gorkhas. On our return in the evening, the drill would be repeated. Sam would

**With the 61 Cavalry polo team, left to right, Majors V.P. Singh, H.S. Sodhi, Raj Kalan and V.S. Sodhi**
Courtesy: 58 Gorkha Training Centre

7 Gardener.
8 The Hindi pronunciation for matches!

With military attachés'
wives on Army Day at the
DSOI, Delhi Cantonment
Courtesy: 58 Gorkha Training Centre

walk through Army House to ensure that the morning's instructions had been carried out. Before
breaking off for the day he would play with his dogs whose dinner bowls would be lined up near
the kitchen wall. Regardless of their pangs of hunger they were not allowed to attack their meal
until Sam pronounced them 'good boys'!

Many ex-servicemen and army widows would stand outside Army House and the chief's
office in South Block hoping for a 'darshan',[9] to petition him on personal matters. One day there
was an important visitor, the wife of his orderly Sher Singh from 4/12 FFR. She had promised
to visit when he became the *'Jangi Lat'*. *'Meri asis si ke Rab tanu Jangi Lat banaye.'* (My
prayer was that God make you the army chief.) True to her word she arrived one morning at
4 King George's Avenue. Sam seated her next to him in the car, took her to his office in South
Block, had a cup of tea with her and spent an hour talking to her. His JCO ADC was then
tasked to escort her to the railway station in his car and make sure she was comfortably seated
on board the train bound for the Punjab.

Sam cared deeply for the veterans of 4/12 FFR and all of us on his staff knew that any burly
Sikh who sought an audience was to be brought to him forthwith regardless of his commitments.
Many of them came like Sher Singh's wife to bask in the glory of seeing their regimental officer

---

9 Audience.

*Sam cared
deeply for the
veterans of
4/12 FFR ...
any burly Sikh
who sought an
audience was
to be brought to
him forthwith
regardless of his
commitments*

On the dance floor
with Silloo
Courtesy: 58 Gorkha Training Centre

*Sam had a
large following
among the press
corps. He made
good copy with
his handsome
looks ... and his
unconventional
sense of humour*

as the *'Jangi Lat'*. Others came to seek a special favour or an intervention. Each veteran would get a patient hearing from the chief before the case was handed over to one of us for redress. The problems ranged from land disputes to non-receipt of pension, from logistical assistance for a wedding in the family to the posting of a relative in the army. Some of the issues were easy to resolve as the mere mention of the army chief's name to a local official was adequate to cut through yards of red tape. But there were requests that verged on the ludicrous, like an out-of-turn promotion for a nephew! It was difficult to make these old soldiers understand why the present *'Jangi Lat'* did not wield the same power as the *'Jangi Lat'* of yore. Dissatisfied, many of them would seek another audience with the chief and, without mincing words, tell him that he had a bunch of incompetents working for him, a message that he gleefully conveyed to us at the first opportunity!

Apart from petitioners there was a never-ending stream of admirers and well-wishers outside Army House. One such regular was Kundan Lal Gujaral, the owner of Moti Mahal, a popular tandoori restaurant in Delhi in the 1960s that had played host to ambassadors, heads of state, film stars and politicians. This gentleman would come laden with frontier delicacies[10] that would invariably be divided between Army House and the ADCs' cottage.

Sam had a large following among the press corps. He made good copy with his handsome looks, his flamboyant personality, his brutal frankness and his unconventional sense of humour.

---

10 Delicacies from the North West Frontier Province.

Among this motley crowd of audience-seekers was a variety of mavericks and astrologers. Sam would occasionally entertain a soothsayer who came highly recommended, but this was mere indulgence for he never set much store by their predictions. In spite of his scepticism, it was a Sikh soothsayer called the 'Kali Kambli', which literally translates as 'person draped in a black blanket', who forecast, much before the 1971 war, that Sam was destined to rise one more rung on the ladder. At the time, this prophecy was interpreted as a possible gubernatorial appointment or an ambassadorship since there were no more rungs left to climb in the army. But the Kali Kambli insisted that he would be promoted *in the army*. Time was to prove him right!

For Sam and Silloo the social circuit in Delhi was demanding; it came with the territory. Apart from army functions, there were National Day celebrations at embassies, invitations from various echelons of government and receptions for visiting foreign dignitaries at Rashtrapati Bhavan.[11] Shortly after Sam became chief, 2/8 GR, on completing its tenure in NEFA, moved to the capital and was garrisoned at the Red Fort with a company at the President's Estate to provide ceremonial and guard duties at Rashtrapati Bhavan and at Army House. Added to Sam's busy calendar were a host of battalion functions. Shubhi and I would alternate to accompany him at social engagements and on tours. For state events, like the president's 'at home', ceremonies at

His charming best with Shubi Har Prashad, wife of VCOAS Lieutenant General 'Nata' Har Prashad
Courtesy: 58 Gorkha Training Centre

Rashtrapati Bhavan, or the opening session of Parliament, both of us were expected to escort him in full military regalia. As aides we were 'on call' round the clock and the phones rang off the hook. We had mastered the art of bouncing out of the deepest sleep to pick up the receiver on hearing the click of the connection even before the ring came through. This should explain why Sam would balk at the thought of a married aide.

In spite of this demanding schedule the chief made sure we had the time to keep up with our physical fitness regimen. Shubhi and I would seize every opportunity to make a dash to the DSOI for a game of squash, a swim, drinks at the bar, followed by dinner. The club was new and membership was instant, but with late hours in the office and the distance from Army House it was not possible to make use of the facilities regularly. To overcome this constraint Sam called the military secretary (MS) to the president and arranged for us to be granted access to the sports facilities at Rashtrapati Bhavan, a stone's throw from Army House.

As we settled down to life in Delhi our social circle grew. We returned hospitality by frequently hosting parties at the cottage. The guest list always included Sam and Silloo.

---

11 The Presidential residence.

*o rrl.∶No/1*

B Bag

HIGH COMMISSION OF INDIA
200 MACLAREN STREET
OTTAWA 4, CANADA

June 18th 1969

My dear Sam,

     I saw a nice picture of you the other day
in one of the Indian newspapers, saying goodbye to K.
This reminded me that I should have written to you
on your assumption of the job of COAS. Good luck to
you. I am sure you won't need any advice from anyone,
particularly from strong minded chaps like myself.
However, one piece of advice I will give you. Have
no pity on your enemies for it is they who will
eventually destroy you.

     I had a letter from Gurchi very recently
and he tells me that the whole army is delighted at
your appointment. I knew this would be so. By the
way, I hope you will keep a kindly eye on Gurchi;
his illness set him back a bit.

     With all good wishes to Siloo and yourself
and I hope to see you some time in December.

Yours ever,

(General J.N. Chaudhuri)

General S. Manekshaw,
Chief of Army Staff,
Army Headquarters,
New Delhi.

Letter of congratulations from General 'Muchu' Chaudhuri (Retd), Indian High Commissioner to Canada
Courtesy: The Manekshaw family

General SHFJ MANEKSHAW, MC DO No 70012/101/COAS

25 June 1969

Thank you very much for your letter No OTT/JNC/1 of 18th June 1969, which I received this morning; it was kind of you to have written and I am most appreciative.

I am settled in your old office and I am at present snowed under trying to understand the background of the various cases; coupled with this I have on my hands Selection Boards — apparently we are still living a hand-to-mouth existence and unless we promote various people there will be lots of Brigadiers appointments lying vacant.

In the home we are quite unsettled and living in the large bed room; it is a bit of a crush, what with one Chief, his wife, a pregnant daughter and five dogs. The rest of the house is in the process of being done up. Coupled with this inconvenience, Delhi is going through a hot spell and lots of dust storms. Tempers are short and the Manekshaws are not on speaking terms with each other most of the time.

I hope you are well and looking after yourself. Incidentally, you still owe me a suit length.

With my warm regards,

S.

Dep Secy
PB. 325

General JN CHAUDHURI
High Commissioner for India
200 Maclaren Street
OTTAWA 4
CANADA

16/1
12/10

Reply from Sam to 'Muchu'
Courtesy: The Manekshaw family

On the morning of the party a choice collection of liquor would arrive from Army House. After a while Swamy, the personal cook, instructed by Sam, would amble over to the cottage and browbeat us into making snacks that showcased his skills rather than our preferences. When the party was in full swing Sam and Silloo would arrive and mix with our guests, mostly young officers and their wives or girlfriends. A few months after our arrival in Delhi I was dating Zenobia and Shubhi was going out with Kavita, the women we would eventually marry. Try as we might to keep this nugget of information from him, Sam sensed there was something more than a mere friendship. He would make it a point to talk to these ladies and extract whatever information he could, egging them on to complain about us. At the right opportunity he would smugly tell us that he knew what we chaps were up to! Sam and Silloo's presence would liven up the party. He would take to the dance floor with our young friends and bowl them over with his charm. After an hour, they would make a discreet exit. The next day we would be grilled: how much liquor had we consumed, who was the young lady with Capt. 'X', what time had we broken off! There were no secrets; we were one big happy family.

The travel commitments of the chief of the army staff are much more onerous than those of an army commander. On tours Sam would take one ADC, an orderly and a civilian PA.[12] Silloo would accompany him sometimes and always displayed the greatest punctuality. Her bags would be packed and outside her room ten minutes before the appointed time. As chief, Sam was flown by the IAF's Communication Squadron.[13] The galley had to be stocked with savouries for all personnel on board and the items had to be purchased from the DSOI. Expenses were billed to the chief's secretariat. During the flight Sam would divide time between his files and talking to personnel on board. At the destination if there was no IAF base, the crew had to be provided with an army liaison officer (LO), accommodation and transport. The IAF loved flying Sam. On our return to Delhi 'thank you' letters to all host formations, including the IAF Communication Squadron, had to be dispatched within twenty-four hours and action on all items he had promised during his tour had to be initiated within forty-eight hours.

Sam made it a point to acquaint himself with each member of his civilian staff. He would walk into their offices to hand over files, stay on for a chat and enquire after their families. When he noticed they were warming their lunch on an electric stove he ordered a food warmer for the office. Sam broke new ground when he included civilian staff in his tour programmes, especially if he was visiting their hometown.

As army chief Sam broke with tradition on two other counts. Discarding the tea and samosa[14] routine, subedar majors whom he hosted on Republic Day were served drinks. 'A subedar sahib does not expect to be served a cup of tea after sundown, that too by his chief!' For the first time JCOs who had received awards on Republic Day were felicitated at the Defence Services Officers' Institute.

---

12 Personal Assistant.

13 The VIP Squadron of the Indian Air Force flies the president, the prime minister, defence minister and the chiefs of the army, the navy and the air force.

14 An Indian savoury.

*When the party was in full swing Sam and Silloo would arrive and mix with our guests, mostly young officers and their wives or girlfriends*

Sam's notations on files and his dexterity with words set off ripples and sometimes tidal waves through Army Headquarters and the Ministry of Defence. Official correspondence used to be routed to and from the defence minister to the army chief through layers of bureaucracy and clerical quagmires (a custom harkening back to the days of the Raj). Files placed on cardboard backing, tied with red tape, which is where the expression 'government red tape' comes from, and covered with a routing sheet that displayed the names of each signatory, would wind their way slowly through the corridors of power. The remarks on files were normally nondescript like 'cleared', 'approved', 'rejected' or 'put up draft to Minister for approval'. I recollect one notation in particular that had me foxed. Sam had received a file with a suggestion from one of his PSOs,[15] a suggestion that to him made no sense. In response he had drawn two circles followed by the letter 's'. Try as I might, I failed to decipher what he had written and eventually went to him to ask what the squiggle meant. He explained that each circle was meant to represent a 'ball' and his doodle aptly conveyed what he thought of the proposal!

After the 1971 victory the Amar Jawan Jyoti, a war memorial to honour soldiers who had laid down their lives, was erected under the canopy of the India Gate. Shortly before inauguration the Home Ministry put up a file to the army chief, suggesting that along with the Armed Forces flag, the BSF[16] flag should also be flown at the memorial. Sam turned down the suggestion with a

---

15 PSOs are principal staff officers to the chief of army staff. These are lieutenant generals who head various directorates at Army Headquarters.
16 Border Security Force.

FROM LEFT TO RIGHT:
Piffer, Kalo and Caesar in the foyer of Army House
Courtesy: 58 Gorkha Training Centre

**ABOVE:**
With ex-servicemen in the Punjab

**RIGHT:**
At the Remount and Veterinary Corps (RVC) Centre, Saharanpur
Courtesy: 58 Gorkha Training Centre

*'The Defence Secretary is but a medium between the Defence Minister and the Chief of Army Staff. It is not his prerogative to ask the Army Chief questions'*

noting that said, 'Fighting and winning wars with external enemies is the task of the Army, Navy and the Air Force and War Memorials worldwide are dedicated to soldiers. The BSF is a police force and nowhere in the world is a War Memorial dedicated to the police.' While Mrs Gandhi had the greatest respect for Khushru Rustomji who raised and commanded the BSF, she stood by Sam's recommendation.

Another time Sam turned down the defence secretary's request for an explanation with the comment, 'The Defence Secretary is but a medium between the Defence Minister and the Chief of Army Staff. It is not his prerogative to ask the Army Chief questions.' The file wound its way through the desk officer to the under secretary, the joint secretary, the additional secretary and finally to the defence secretary. Within minutes the latter was in the chief's office, file in hand, requesting him to expunge his comment. Sam stood his ground, making it abundantly clear that in the future the secretary should think twice before asking him for an explanation. The bureaucrats quickly learnt that this army chief could not be trifled with.

Sam's reputation as a fair administrator opened the floodgates to a large number of officers seeking justice. Some of the grievances he was asked to adjudicate were personal and verged on the ridiculous as was the case of a captain from the Brigade of Guards, a north Indian who happened to be madly in love with the daughter of a colonel from the RVC,[17] a south Indian. The colonel had repeatedly turned down the captain's proposal for his daughter's hand in marriage and the desperate young officer approached his chief. Sam convinced the colonel that the young officer was outstanding, the proverbial needle in the haystack. The colonel had such high regard for Sam's judgement that he relented and the young couple tied the knot a few months later.

17 Remount and Veterinary Corps.

ABOVE:
**Inspecting the Quarterguard
at the RVC Centre**

LEFT:
**Briefing on Key Location
Plan (KLP) at 14 GTC,
Sabathu (Simla hills)**
Courtesy: 58 Gorkha Training Centre

Several times a day Sam would walk into the office that Shubhi and I shared. If he found us tucking into samosas, he'd perch on the edge of our desks and partake of the feast. One morning he entered our office and found a lieutenant from the Armoured Corps in our room. He asked the young man what brought him to his ADCs' office. 'Nothing, Sir,' stuttered the nervous officer, 'I just dropped by.' 'No one comes to see my ADCs for nothing. Beroze, bring this young man to my office.' When Sam got to know that the officer wanted to resign his commission, he rang the military secretary, Maj. Gen. Sarkar, 'Jimmy, I have a youngster in my office who does not want to serve under me. Please make sure that he gets out of my army.' He turned to the officer and said, 'Boy, out you go!' The officer was out of the room in a flash and out of uniform a week later.

In spite of his busy schedule Sam made time for his hobbies. Army House had a Jersey cow, poultry, an apiary and a vegetable patch. His household staff could purchase the produce at nominal rates while milk was supplied free for children and pregnant mothers. The garden received his personal attention. He would be up at the crack of dawn tending a variety of exotic roses purchased from the Pusa Institute. The flowerbeds were always a riot of colour and in winter his chrysanthemum blooms were showstoppers.

Sam also found the time to potter around the kitchen and try his hand at his Parsi favourites like *'dodhi no morabbo'* (white pumpkin preserve), *'eedan pak'* (a savoury of eggs and cream) and *'kharya ni jelly'* (jelly made from trotters). His forays into the kitchen were never devoid of loud bickering with Swamy, who did not appreciate invasion of his territory. Silloo wisely distanced herself from these pursuits!

Sam had a passion for music and his prized possession was a complex audio system in his bedroom that comprised of an assortment of turntables, tape recorders, amplifiers and speakers connected through a maze of wires. Sam had a great collection of music and if you dropped the

*In spite of his busy schedule Sam made time for his hobbies ... The garden received his personal attention*

slightest hint of appreciation, the next day he would present you with a cassette that he would make the time to record himself. One day his music system stopped working and try as they might technicians from leading music shops in Delhi could not put it back on the rails. Someone suggested that the services of Maj. Oswyn 'Ossie' Pereira (Corps of Signals), a consummate genius in the field, be requisitioned. Ossie was quick to identify and correct the problem much to Sam's relief. Finally, here was the man he had been looking for all these years. But Ossie had applied for immigration to the UK and a few weeks later his papers came through. When this news travelled up the grapevine to Sam, Ossie was again summoned to Army House and given a sound dressing down. How could he desert his chief and abandon him to his fate? Ossie stood there like a good soldier and allowed Sam to rant. The next day he was summoned for a third time to Army House but this time he was presented with a bottle of Scotch and a silver khukri[18] with the army chief's best wishes for his new endeavour. With Ossie's departure all we could do was cross our fingers and hope for the best.

The staff at Army House comprised of two Gorkha orderlies, a civilian *mali*, a dhobi[19] and Swamy. Come 7.00 pm and staff and families would troop into the foyer of Army House and

18 A curved Gorkha dagger. In this case an ornamental one with a carved silver sheath.
19 Washerman.

squat on a *durrie*[20] in front of the television set to watch Indian soaps and movies. Visitors who came calling had to pick their way through this assembly as best as they could. The TV was one of three gifted to Sam by his close friend, Sir Padampat Singhania, the owner of JK Industries. One was retained in Army House for the staff, one was sent to the ADCs' cottage and one was given to the MA.

Swamy was the longest-serving member of the household staff. He had been with the family since Sam's posting as the commandant of the Staff College in 1959. The Manekshaws took him and his family under their wing, securing a job for one son as a clerk with the Staff College and for another as a driver with the American embassy in Delhi. Swamy and Sam loved to spar over trivia. Each morning Sam would spell out the menu for the day and each evening on return from office, he would swing by the kitchen and needle Swamy by opening his pots and pans and criticising his cooking. One day Silloo was returning to Delhi after a month in England where she'd gone to babysit grandson Raoul-Sam while Maja was taking her Bar exams. Sam teased Swamy, speaking in the same broken English that Swamy spoke, 'Madam coming back tonight, I telling Madam you lousy cook, not feeding me well for one month.' Not one to be outdone, Swamy replied, 'Yes,

FACING PAGE:
**Army House garden in full bloom**

**Sam playing Holi at Army House. To the extreme right is Colonel Girdhari Lal**
Courtesy: 58 Gorkha Training Centre

20 Cotton carpet.

Madam coming back tonight, I telling Madam you not eating at home for one month. Going out every night and coming home at 1 o'clock in the morning!' Sam stomped out of the kitchen with a mock display of annoyance, 'You damn cook. Is that how you talk to the Army Chief!' And Swamy would insist on having the last word, 'Yes, now you big man, you Army Chief. You go look after your Army and leave my kitchen!'

Sam had an eclectic assortment of friends. Mr L.N. Mishra, minister of foreign trade, was a frequent visitor. He would drop by Army House to confide in Sam and use him as a sounding board for his political manoeuvring. The indirect beneficiaries of this friendship were Shubhi and I. Sam was able to get us Fiat cars within weeks from the ministerial quota in the days when the waiting period for a car could be up to two years.

Another frequent visitor at Army House was Mr Sanwal Bhalotia, a simple Marwari businessman from Calcutta for whom Silloo was a 'Mem'.[21] Sanwal was a man of considerable wealth who was wary of going abroad, but each time Sam returned from a visit, he would grill him with questions about the trip. Just before our visit to Russia Sanwal dropped in one evening and Sam asked if he could bring him a gift from the USSR. Sanwal had no attraction for foreign goods,

*Each morning Sam would spell out the menu for the day and each evening ... he would swing by the kitchen and needle Swamy by ... criticising his cooking*

---

21 The Indian nomenclature for a British lady during the days of the Raj.

**With subedar majors posted at Army HQ during an 'at home' at Army House in January 1970**
Courtesy: 58 Gorkha Training Centre

so he thanked Sam but politely turned down the offer. Sam persisted and knowing Sanwal was a shy man, he teased, '*Accha, kutch nahi to Russian Mem ley aaoon tere liye?*' (If nothing, should I bring you a Russian girl?) The poor man was so embarrassed that he beat a hasty retreat to the safe haven of his home.

Every few months, the Manekshaws would host a cocktail party for household and office staff. The guest list included Lt Col. Depinder Singh and his wife, Balli, Shubhi and I, Kavita and Zenobia (honorary members as our prospective wives), Maj. and Mrs Girdhari Lal, the subedar

**SAM CREATES PRECEDENT**

# JCOs FETED AT OFFICERS' CLUB

YET another tradition in the Army towards fraternisation between officers and other ranks was broken on Tuesday evening when Chief of the Army Staff S. H. F. J. Manekshaw accorded a reception to the winners of distinguished awards at the Defence Services Officers Institute in New Delhi reports PTI.

It was the first time that Junior Commissioned Officers, and a Lance-Naik were invited to this exclusively officers' club since it was established seven years ago.

Gen Manekshaw had broken a tradition soon after he took over as the Army Chief when he served drinks to the JCOs at the annual Army Day reception held at the Army House in January 1970. Earlier only tea and refreshments used to be served at this reception.

## SINGLE FILE

On that occasion Gen Manekshaw also changed a long-standing practice. Earlier the senior JCO guests used to wait on the pavement outside the Army House till the time scheduled for the reception and then march single file into the house and the lawns, to be received by the Army Chief.

In the 1970 reception, the senior JCOs walked into the house as they came along and were received by the Army Chief's aides. Later the Army Chief received them as they walked into the lawns and had them drinks offered. He mixed with them clinking glasses.

Ordinarily the only occasion when the officers, including the Army Chief, share drinks with the JCOs and other ranks is during the bara khanas (common feasts). But even on these occasions there is no fraternisation. The distinctions of ranks are observed.

TOP:
News clipping on his breaking with tradition

LEFT:
Sam's doodle during a high-powered meeting
Courtesy: The Manekshaw family

HIGH LEVEL PLANNING
DEPICTED
PICTORIALLY

"HIGHER THE LEVEL BIGGER THE BALLS"

major ADC, civilian staff officers, clerks and peons from the chief's secretariat, drivers, Swamy, the Gorkhas, the dhobi, the *mali* and their families. A long table would be laid in the driveway of Army House. Rum and soft drinks and Swamy's snacks would comprise the menu. The party would last for a couple of hours. After the first few drinks knocked back in quick succession the dhobi would be under the table. His wife, the *dhoban*, was a pretty woman, always glamorously turned out. After one such party Sam joked that each year the *dhoban* produced a child that strangely enough resembled one or the other of his Gorkhas! ◆

Visit to US Army Armor
Center, Fort Knox,
Kentucky

**FACING PAGE:**
Guard of Honour at
Shremetyevo International
Airport, Moscow

Courtesy: 58 Gorkha Training Centre

# Visits and Visitors

As the chief of army staff, Sam visited several countries. The first invitation he received was from the USA. It was forwarded to the Ministry of Defence for approval. The visit was cleared but with a caveat; Sam was authorised to fly first class but the rest of the delegation, including Silloo, was restricted to economy class. Sam returned the file to the ministry saying he would regret the invitation, stating explicitly that he would rather forgo the visit than expect his wife to travel in the tail of the aircraft. A nervous bureaucrat, realising this was no idle threat, put the file up to the prime minister for a final decision. She overruled the ministry and thereafter Silloo flew first class with him on all official trips.

In April 1970, accompanied by Maj. Gen. Gurbachan Singh, GOC 1st Armoured Division and Capt. Shubhi Sood, Sam and Silloo visited the US. In Washington DC, he met with the top brass of the US Army at the Pentagon, with senators on Capitol Hill and laid a wreath at the Tomb of the Unknown Soldier at the Arlington National Cemetery. He was presented with the US Legion of Merit award given to armed forces personnel for extraordinary meritorious conduct in the discharge of duties and outstanding achievements. The delegation then flew to Fort Bragg, North

**Legion of Merit award**
Courtesy: 58 Gorkha Training Centre

Carolina, to witness a demonstration on rapid deployment by the XVIII Airborne Corps and to Fort Campbell, Kentucky, for a demonstration on air assault by the 101st Airborne Division, the 'Screaming Eagles'. When Sam returned from the US, I was at the airport to receive him. He handed me a small Philips music system that he had carried as hand baggage, knowing this was one item my room lacked.

In September 1970, at the invitation of Marshal Grechko, the Soviet defence minister, Sam visited the (erstwhile) USSR accompanied by Silloo. Maj. Gen. J.F.R. Jacob (Artillery), Chief of Staff, Eastern Command, was his general-in-waiting and I accompanied him as his aide.

In Moscow, there were meetings at Defence HQ, a wreath-laying ceremony at the Tomb of the Unknown Soldier, visits to the Red Square, the Kremlin, Lenin's mausoleum, St Basil's cathedral and the Memorial Museum of Astronautics dedicated to space exploration. We were taken to the famous Tamanski Division on the outskirts of Moscow. It was a vast complex housing Russia's 'constant readiness' division that can be deployed at short notice during political crises. We spent two days in Leningrad (now St Petersburg), which gave us a unique opportunity to see the rich culture and architectural marvels of tsarist Russia.

This was followed by a three-day visit to an armoured formation in Kiev, the capital of Ukraine, to witness a firepower demonstration by T-54 tanks that the Indian Army purchased from the USSR. We spent the next morning walking the length and breadth of the ordnance factory that manufactured these tanks. In the afternoon we were taken to a farm owned by an old lady who had been awarded the 'Star of the Soviet Union' for growing potatoes to feed the Russian Army during WWII. We walked another few miles on her farm after which she invited us to her house and served us home-brewed vodka. The day was not yet done. That evening we were taken to a theatre to watch a ballet performance. As the lights dimmed and we sank into cushioned chairs, the lilting music and the lashings of vodka made it hard for the chief and me to keep our eyes open. Our Russian hosts were not a bit perturbed by our philistine behaviour but Silloo was on pins and needles and was barely able to enjoy the performance as she spent the entire evening elbowing Sam and me, sitting on either side of her, whenever our snoring went an octave too high.

We returned to Moscow, to more meetings, more vodka, more dinners and of course more cultural shows. Theatre did not seem to sit well with us; we were no great aficionados of ballet and would have preferred to explore the city on our feet. In fact, Maj. Gen. Jacob (Jake) thought he could steal a march on our Russian hosts. After the ballet performance, he had made arrangements to spend the rest of the evening with an officer from his regiment who was attending the all-arms tactical course in Moscow. He was looking forward to a night out and a visit to some local bars. A few minutes before the curtain came down and the lights came on, 'Jake' disappeared, but his euphoria was short-lived. Our Russian LO detained the entire delegation at the theatre until the truant general was located and brought to heel. After all personnel had been accounted for, we were escorted back to the hotel. Our visit was during the communist era and although we were treated most graciously we were kept under discreet surveillance with no latitude to explore the city unsupervised. One evening we had a gap in an otherwise very busy schedule and wanted to walk around the Red Square and St Basil's. When we requested the liaison officer for transport, he did not refuse but with a combination of delaying tactics and excuses he was able to thwart our plans. We spent two hours confined in the hotel, sorely disappointed. However, the Russians did compensate, for they took us to the wonderful holiday resort of Crimea.

In Russia, wherever we went, my Gorkha hat drew a great deal of admirers. Women and children wanted to pose for photographs with me, ignoring the army chief and holding up the delegation. Eventually, Sam had to take a potshot at me, 'Beroze, every dog has his day and today is yours!' We returned to India after a three-day vacation in Rome including a visit to the exotic Isle of Capri.

A month later I again accompanied the COAS, this time to erstwhile Yugoslavia. Our host was Gen. Viktor Bubanj, Chief of General Staff, Yugoslav People's Army. At the time India and

*... Silloo ... spent the entire evening elbowing Sam and me, sitting on either side of her, whenever our snoring went an octave too high*

**Visit to Pope Air Force Base, North Carolina**
Courtesy: 58 Gorkha Training Centre

TASHICHHODZONG
THIMPHU

August 12, 1972.

His Majesty the King of Bhutan

Dear General,

I am most grateful to you for your kind letter of good
wishes on my accession to the Throne of the Kingdom of Bhutan.
I am aware of the close bonds of affection and understanding
which existed between my beloved father and yourself. The
Indian Army under your dynamic leadership has made a great
contribution to the security of Bhutan. I have no doubt that
the present happy relations between the Indian Army and my
government will not only be maintained but further strengthened
in the years to come. I know that you will extend the same
friendship and co-operation to me as you did to my father, and
that you will not hesitate to let me have the benefit of your
wise counsel on all matters affecting the security of our two
countries.

with highest personal regards,

yours sincerely,

( J. S. Wangchuck )

General SHFJ Manekshaw, MC,
Army Headquarters,
New Delhi - 11.

**Letter from the young king
of Bhutan**
Courtesy: The Manekshaw family

*Sam's visits to
the kingdoms
of Bhutan
and Sikkim
were more like
'homecoming'
... harkening
back to his
days as
eastern army
commander*

Yugoslavia were members of the Non-Aligned Movement. The cordiality with which we were received by the general and his PSOs was palpable. The delegation was taken to military outposts along the Austrian border and places of tourist interest, including a famous crystal factory on the outskirts of Belgrade. At the end of the visit Sam returned to Delhi while Silloo and I spent a week in London with Maja.

In November 1971 Sam visited the USSR again. It was during the build-up to the Indo-Pak war, with the clear objective of making good the shortfall of equipment. I was with my battalion, deployed in the Rajasthan sector. Shubhi accompanied Sam on this trip. There was tension between India and Pakistan and adversarial rhetoric was at an all-time high. Shubhi recounts that the delegation was taken to the Bolshoi Theatre where Sam chanced upon Jamsheed Marker, Pakistan's ambassador to the USSR, and his wife Diana. Jamsheed is from Quetta and Sam's friendship with Jamsheed and his family went back to his days as a student at the Staff College in 1943. They greeted each other with a bear hug and Sam planted a kiss on each of Diana's cheeks in true Parsi style. They spent a few minutes exchanging pleasantries in Gujarati, their mother tongue. This had the Russians thoroughly perplexed as the behaviour of Pakistan's ambassador and India's army chief was totally out of sync with the atmosphere of animosity between the two countries!

In 1972 Sam visited Nepal at the invitation of the Nepalese army chief. Sam and Silloo were granted an audience with King Birendra and Queen Aishwarya. Before the meeting the Indian ambassador briefed them on Nepalese protocol. They were expected to speak to the royals only when spoken to. Sam heeded the advice for the first half hour and was guarded and correct, but he must have found the atmosphere stifling for during an awkward, long pause in the conversation he turned to the queen and in a most casual manner asked if the king was a good husband and helped her with chores in the kitchen. Queen Aishwarya burst out laughing and the royals themselves threw protocol to the wind. Sam's visits to the kingdoms of Bhutan and Sikkim were more like 'homecoming'. He had a special relationship with the *chogyal* of Sikkim and King Jigme Singhe Wangchuck of Bhutan, harkening back to his days as eastern army commander.

In February 1971, Gen. W.C. Westmoreland, Chief of Staff of the US Army, accepted an invitation to visit India. The first stop for the American delegation was Jaipur with the Rajasthan royal family playing host. Next was a visit to an armoured division in Jhansi. Since the general was a keen polo player, the division had organised a polo match on bicycles instead of horses. Gen. Westmoreland may have had some initial reservations but these were soon laid to rest for the hosts had carefully choreographed the game and the chief guest scored the winning goal. The next stop was Sikkim. Sam wanted Gen. Westmoreland to visit this beautiful kingdom and meet

1. Laying a wreath at the Tomb of the Unknown Soldier

2. The Bhutan army chief calling on Sam

3. Presenting a model of the Indian Vijayanta tank to General Viktor Bubanj, Chief of General Staff of (erstwhile) Yugoslav People's Army

4. Greeting the *chogyal* of Sikkim

5. General Westmoreland being introduced to Indian soldiers at Delhi airport on arrival in India

Courtesy: 58 Gorkha Training Centre

1. At Leningrad

2. Being received at Tribhuvan International Airport, Kathmandu

3. Welcoming General F. Jam, Chief of the Supreme Commander's Staff of the Imperial Iranian Armed Forces

4. Receiving Major General Idi Amin of the Ugandan Army at Palam airport, New Delhi

5. Hosting General Viktor Bubanj and his wife at the DSOI, Delhi Cantonment

6. At the Memorial Museum of Astronautics

Courtesy: 58 Gorkha Training Centre

the *chogyal* and his American wife, Hope Cook, but more importantly, he was proud to showcase the arduous conditions under which his soldiers kept vigil in the inhospitable, high-altitude terrain along the border with China. Gen. Westmoreland was duly impressed with the morale and motivation of the Indian soldiers he met everywhere, from the deserts of Rajasthan to the gruelling heights of the Himalayas and he acknowledged what a fine job the Indian Army was doing.

Other generals who visited India while Sam was chief were Gen. Viktor Bubanj, of the erstwhile Yugoslav People's Army and Gen. Fereydoun Jam, chief of the Imperial Iranian Armed Forces. Gen. Bubanj was taken on a tour of Eastern Command, primarily to Nathu-La in Sikkim while Gen. Jam was taken to the Parachute Regimental Centre at Agra and the Infantry School, Mhow.

In 1972 Sam was invited to visit Iran. Unfortunately, the trip had to be aborted after our luggage had reached the airport because of the urgency to settle outstanding border issues with Pakistan after the 1971 war. Instead of Tehran the next morning we were headed for Lahore, but I will come to that in due course.

The most colourful military officer who visited India was Maj. Gen. Idi Amin, commander of the Ugandan Army. This was in the summer of 1970, prior to his seizing power through a coup in January 1971 and his insane autocracy, although even then he had all the makings of a maverick. On the last night of his visit, the army chief hosted a dinner in his honour at the Ashoka Hotel in Delhi. An hour into the function Idi Amin told Sam that he was impressed with the Indian Army uniform and would like to take back a dozen sets for himself. This created a major crisis. The owner of a famous tailoring shop, Eddies, in Connaught Place, was requested to come to the army's rescue. Bales of olive green material were put at his disposal and more than a dozen tailors laboured through the night. The next day Idi Amin returned to Kampala, carrying twelve sets of uniforms with him. Thankfully, there was no invitation for a return visit for by then the man had gone off the deep end.

The visit that Sam cherished most was from his ex-boss and last British C-in-C, Gen. Sir Roy Bucher. Sam had served under him as DMO and as a parting gift Gen. Bucher had given him an autographed photograph that said, 'To Sam, one of the best staff officers I have ever met.' Accompanied by his wife, he made a nostalgic journey to India in January 1970 and stayed at Army House. Although this was a personal visit, Sam informed the government and Gen. Bucher was honoured as an official guest at the Beating of the Retreat[1] ceremony at Vijay Chowk (Victory Square) on January 29. ◆

**Inspecting a Guard of Honour presented by soldiers of the Bhutan Army**
Courtesy: 58 Gorkha Training Centre

*The visit that Sam cherished most was from his ex-boss and last British C-in-C, Gen. Sir Roy Bucher*

---

1 A military ceremony performed by the massed bands of the army, navy and air force to mark the end of Republic Day celebrations.

Morale boosting. Visiting troops in forward areas just before the war. With him is Lieutenant General Sartaj Singh, GOC 15 Corps

FACING PAGE:
On an Armored Personnel Carrier (APC)
Courtesy: 58 Gorkha Training Centre

# The 1971 War

1971 brought with it ominous forebodings of war on the Indian subcontinent. In 1970 the Awami League, an East Pakistan political party, won a majority of seats in Pakistan's federal elections, marginalising Zulfikar Ali Bhutto's Pakistan People's Party of West Pakistan. This made Sheikh Mujibur Rehman, a Bengali Muslim and the leader of the Awami League, the top contender for the post of prime minister of Pakistan. Prior to that, in 1966 Mujib had proposed a six-point plan for the autonomy of East Pakistan. West Pakistanis and Mr Bhutto viewed this as secession and rejected it outright. Even after winning a clear majority in 1970, the Sheikh was not invited to form the government. This sparked a civil disobedience movement in East Pakistan, and the president and chief marshal law administrator, Gen. Yahya Khan, ordered army action. A military crackdown began on March 25, 1971 and in the early hours of March 26 Mujib was arrested from his home in Dacca and flown to West Pakistan. The next day, on March 27, Maj. Ziaur Rahman, on behalf of Sheikh Mujib, declared independence of the sovereign 'Republic of Bangladesh' from Pakistan and the eastern half of the country ceased to exist. News of Mujib's arrest

LEFT TO RIGHT:
The three service chiefs,
Air Chief Marshal P.C.
Lal, Admiral 'Charles'
Nanda and General Sam
Manekshaw with Defence
Minister Babu Jagjivan Ram
Courtesy: 58 Gorkha Training Centre

*Sam stood his ground. The knee-jerk reaction of the government and the proposal emanating from the cabinet was completely flawed*

spread and East Pakistan went up in flames as political protests and agitations raged. Gen. Tikka Khan was sent to quell the uprising. This resulted in civil war as Bengali officers in the Pakistan Army and soldiers of the East Bengal Rifles deserted and formed the 'Mukti Bahini' or 'Liberation Army'. Tikka launched 'Operation Searchlight'. Thousands of intellectuals in universities were killed in pogroms and protestors were mercilessly butchered, creating a humanitarian crisis. In the months that followed, waves of refugees, totalling over ten million, poured into India and the economic, financial and logistical burden on the border states of West Bengal, Assam and Tripura became non-sustainable. Repeated appeals by India to Pakistan to rein in the military action against unarmed civilians fell on deaf ears and the influx of these displaced persons finally became inimical to peace in the region.

Towards the end of April 1971, after all attempts at diplomacy had failed, the army chief was invited to a cabinet meeting. The prime minister and her cabinet wanted the army to launch an immediate offensive against Pakistan. Sam stood his ground. The knee-jerk reaction of the government and the proposal emanating from the cabinet was completely flawed. Spelling out facts that were germane to any military planning he queried the impulse to jump the gun. The timing was not right. He needed time to mobilise formations to their operational locations and ensure adequate and uninterrupted logistical support. This would entail requisitioning trains, railway wagons, trucks and civilian aircraft. Crops were ready to be harvested in the Punjab and the diversion of rolling stock would result in food shortages. To ensure uninterrupted reinforcements and supplies to forward locations, additional roads would need to be built by the Border Roads Organisation (BRO). Logistically, any operation in summer spelt disaster with the entire delta region of West Bengal turning into a vast swamp with the monsoon rains. This would confine the movement of armoured vehicles to the roads and expose his plans to the enemy. Air support would be restricted because of poor visibility. Any entry into East Pakistan would be suicidal until the rivers had ebbed and the snow had blocked any chance of the Chinese opening up a third front along the northern border. The army was not adequately equipped. The Armoured Division had just eleven tanks in operational condition out of 189; requisitions for purchase were pending with the Ministry of Finance. Sam refused to be bulldozed into a misadventure. Referring to the routing of the Indian Army in 1962 by the Chinese, Sam is believed to have said to Mrs Gandhi, 'Madam Prime Minister, you may not mind being in the same position as your father was in 1962 but I certainly don't want to be in the position that he [the army chief] was.'[1] A very grim prime minister dismissed the cabinet but asked Sam to stay back. Soldiers are meant to obey orders, but as senior officers they have a moral responsibility to stand up to politicians when they issue directives that are ill-conceived and impractical to execute without jeopardising the lives of the

**The army chief in the driver's seat**
Courtesy: 58 Gorkha Training Centre

1 Courtesy: Lt Gen. A.M. Vohra in his write-up on Field Marshal Sam Manekshaw.

**Pep talk, victory shall
be ours**
Courtesy: 58 Gorkha Training Centre

men they command. Sensing her anger he asked, '… would you like me to send in my resignation on grounds of health, mental or physical?' 'Sit down, Sam. Is everything you told me true?' 'Yes, it is my job to tell you the truth.' If war was the option of last resort, it would be at his call. 'It is my job to fight and it is my job to win.' He assured the prime minister that East Pakistan would capitulate within a month, but only if he was given a free hand, if the timing was of his choice, and if he had only one political master to report to, the prime minister. She agreed to his terms of engagement. While this strategy served the army and the country well, it did not sit well with the defence minister, Babu Jagjivan Ram, and Sam paid the price for that later. Narrating this, while delivering a lecture at the DSSC on November 11, 1998 on 'Leadership and Discipline', he said that on that day he had successfully walked the fine line 'between becoming a field marshal and being dismissed!'

With that the planning of the most brilliant campaign in military history began. Preparation and coordination with departments of government and ministries commenced. The army chief and representatives of key ministries met weekly to track progress. For the first month the civil administration continued to drag its feet which left Sam with no option but to convey his frustration to the prime minister; he was losing valuable time. The next meeting was held in the Ops Room of Army Headquarters. Sam summed up the situation: progress had been glacial.

The Finance Ministry was yet to approve expenditures and release funds to line ministries. The army was awaiting approval from the Defence Ministry to make up deficiencies. The railways had reneged on all deadlines; work on extending the railheads up to the borders had not commenced nor had rolling stock been released, holding up the movement of troops and material. A furious prime minister turned on her ministers. Each of them was made to commit to a deadline and with that the preparations for war commenced in earnest.

BRO engineers worked round the clock to construct roads and bridges to facilitate swift and deep penetration into enemy lines and to maintain the supply chain. Equipment deficiencies were identified and plugged through accelerated imports, mainly from the USSR. Depots for POL,[2] ration, equipment, arms and ammunition were established at forward points, within easy reach of the war zones. Plans were recalibrated to launch an attack on the eastern front and conduct a 'holding operation' in the west. In May 1971 Maj. Gen. Onkar Singh Kalkat (8 GR) was posted to Eastern Command as director of operations to train and equip the Mukti Bahini and to oversee its operations. During the war this ancillary force did an outstanding job of disrupting the Pakistan Army's logistical bases and communication facilities in East Pakistan. Through continuous forays into their defence lines, it achieved the objective of downgrading force levels and their battle worthiness. Sam kept the prime minister posted on planning and progress.

---

2 Petrol, oil and lubricants.

*... on that day he [Sam] had successfully walked the fine line 'between becoming a field marshal and being dismissed!'*

**A mug of tea and a joke**
Courtesy: 58 Gorkha Training Centre

*In the month of August [1971], the Indian Armed Forces were put on full alert ... and all personnel were told to report to their units*

'I stand with you.' In a trench at a FDL
Courtesy: 58 Gorkha Training Centre

In August 1971 Mrs Gandhi launched a diplomatic blitzkrieg, touring the US, UK and other western nations to express India's concern at the military crackdown by the Pakistan Army on the unarmed people of East Pakistan that had resulted in a non-sustainable influx of refugees into India for the last six months. If the UN and world community did not rein in Pakistan, India would be left with no option but to resolve the problem militarily. To counter American and Chinese support to Pakistan, India signed a twenty-year Treaty of Peace, Friendship and Cooperation with the USSR. The main proviso was that in case of imminent threat they would '... enter into mutual consultations ... and take appropriate effective measures to ensure the peace and security of their countries.' The immediate advantage of the treaty was that the Indian Army was able to make up its deficiencies, especially of tanks. It also resulted in strong political support from the Soviets once the war got underway. The USSR repeatedly vetoed motions for ceasefire at the UN Security Council, which gave the Indian Army the extra time it needed to accomplish its mission. Leonid Brezhnev, the general secretary of the Communist Party of the Soviet Union, ordered forty divisions of the Russian Army to mobilise along the border with China, thereby thwarting any Chinese plans to support Pakistan by opening up another front for India in the north. Sam had laid much of the groundwork for this during his visit to the Soviet Union.

In the month of August, the Indian Armed Forces were put on full alert. Training courses were cut short, leave was cancelled and all personnel were told to report to their units. Trains and civil aircraft were requisitioned and formations were mobilised to their operational locations.

I had a difficult decision to make. If I continued as aide to the army chief I would have the unique opportunity to see the execution of war at the highest level of command. On the other hand, I did not want to be marked as an officer who had dodged war. After pondering this for a while I approached Sam with trepidation, mindful of jumping ship when he most needed two aides. Without a moment's hesitation he supported my decision to join my battalion. A few weeks later I was at Delhi junction in my battle fatigues, on my way to Anupgarh in Rajasthan with 2/8 GR. I boarded the military special, excited and hopeful to see combat action that I had trained for. We reached our 'op location'[3] under 11 Corps, dug our

---

3 Operational location.

Briefing on the bonnet
of a jeep by a brigade
commander. Behind him
are Lieutenant General
Navin Rawlley, GOC 11
Corps, and his deputy
MA, Major Shubhi Sood
Courtesy: 58 Gorkha Training Centre

defences in shifting sands, familiarised with the terrain and went through repeated 'drills' in preparation for D-Day. As a young captain I was in the first line of defence.

In October we were informed of the army chief's visit to 11 Corps. A day prior to his arrival I was ordered by my CO to be present at the helipad; the chief had expressed a desire to meet me. Corps Commander Lt Gen. Navin Rawlley was there to receive Sam and drive him to forward locations. I was ordered to accompany them. When the chopper landed I was present in full battle order[4] with my loaded sten machine carbine (SMC). Sam commented that I looked pretty darn good; life in the desert and trenches seemed to sit well with me! We took off in a Willys jeep with the corps commander at the wheel, me at the other end of the long front seat while the army chief sat jammed between us. Willys jeeps were not particularly spacious vehicles and my left leg was propped outside on the footboard while I clutched the SMC between my knees. This weapon had a very poor safety record and the slightest jerk could set off a volley of bullets. As we sped along the bumpy track, Sam turned to me and said, 'Beroze, can you hold that damn thing on the outside. You don't want to be court-martialled for firing on your Chief, do you?' I quickly switched the position of the weapon! Each time we arrived at an FDL we confused the army brass; for instead of the chief of army staff stepping

---

4 Battle dress.

out 'kerb side' as per protocol, the officials were surprised to see a captain in full battle order emerge from the jeep, followed by the army chief!

I must transgress here to highlight Sam's concern for his staff and their families. Prior to this visit he had called Zenobia at IBM, 'Sweetie, I'm going to visit Beroze. Would you like to send something for the bugger?' On his return he called again, 'The blighter is doing well except *karo thikra jevo thai gayoch* (he's turned dark as pitch). If he wants to come back and work for me *thikroo ghasvoo parse* (he'll have to scrub off the grime). You don't worry about him, sleep well.' Zenobia's colleagues were amazed that the COAS while planning a war had the time and concern to ring his ADC's girlfriend and reassure her that all was well.

Sam visited all formations on the front to ensure preparedness and to motivate his men. His very presence was electrifying. Addressing troops in simple language he spelt out his expectations. 'A soldier's business is to fight and win battles not to rape and loot. When you enter Pakistan, treat the women with respect like your mothers and sisters. Anyone who disobeyed orders will be court-martialled. I am commanding soldiers, not thieves.' His words had a profound impact on the men who were primed for battle.

With formation commanders Sam was much tougher. Truth should not become a casualty of war. He expected honest reporting of gains and losses. He would accept an error of judgement but any formation commander who deliberately misinformed him regarding the ground reality would be sacked forthwith. Nor would he condone rape, but to his officers this directive was conveyed in true Manekshaw style, 'If you feel an urge, if you feel tempted, put your hands in your pockets and think of Sam Manekshaw.'

Sam issued orders that all messages and directives of MO Directorate and all documents and correspondence pertaining to the war, however inconsequential they might seem, should not be removed or destroyed. He wanted to ensure that records were maintained for posterity.

On November 30, Maj. Gen. Inder Gill, officiating DMO, received a call from the Australian Military Attaché in Delhi. Families of diplomats in Islamabad were being evacuated, a clear indication that Pakistan was priming to strike. Four days later, on December 3, 1971 at 3.50 pm the Pakistan Air Force strafed eleven Indian airfields on the western front from Srinagar to Jodhpur, including the air base at Agra, 201 km east of New Delhi. The prime minister, who was in Calcutta, was informed and the government alerted. Orders were issued to strike back by land, by air and by sea and with that India and Pakistan went to war for the third time since Independence.

The Indian Army, along with the Mukti Bahini, launched a three-prong attack on East Pakistan. The enemy forces were

Pamphlet calling on Pakistani troops to surrender

## Officers and Jawans of the Pakistan Army

Indian Forces have surrounded you. Your Air Force is destroyed. You have no hope of any help from them. Chittagong, Chalna and Mangla ports are blocked. Nobody can reach you from the sea. Your fate is sealed. The Mukti Bahini and the people are all prepared to take revenge for the atrocities and cruelties you have committed... Why waste lives? Don't you want to go home to be with your children? Do not lose time; there is no disgrace in laying down your arms to a soldier. We will give you the treatment befitting a soldier.

outnumbered and outflanked. Pakistan ground forces could get no support from their air force since the Dacca airfield had been strafed and twenty aircraft on the tarmac were destroyed. The Indian Navy had blockaded the Bay of Bengal, making sure that no reinforcements could reach by sea. In an orchestrated move, rumours were spread that India intended to launch a major assault on Dacca. On December 11 two Caribou aircraft, with 'dummies' dressed like paratroopers, lifted off from Agra. The Pakistan Army was conned into believing that the entire Parachute Brigade had been deployed while in actual fact only the 2nd Parachute Battalion, commanded by Lt Col. K.S. Pannu, was dropped at Tangail in East Pakistan and ordered to march on and surround Dacca. Pakistani troops were taken by surprise and abandoned their positions. Alarmed at the rapid gains made by the Indian Army, Maj. Gen. Rao Farman Ali, military advisor to the governor general of East Pakistan, lost his nerve and approached the UN Security Council for a ceasefire. Message intercepts between Pakistani generals indicated that their army was on the verge of capitulating. Sam had it all down to the wire. As soon as he got word that our troops had surrounded Dacca, he went on the airwaves, calling on Pakistani soldiers to lay down their arms. Pamphlets of his speech, translated into Urdu, Punjabi, Pashto and Bengali, the languages spoken by Pakistani soldiers, were dropped over East Pakistan. The impact of this message from no less a person than the Indian army chief demoralised the Pakistan forces further and, according to defence analysts, is supposed to have shortened the war by two weeks.

Sam's strategy worked, for on December 14 he received a message through the US embassy and the UNDP representative in Delhi, the two principal interlocutors for the Pakistan Army, that Lt Gen. A.A.K. Niazi, commander of the Pakistani forces in East Pakistan, was prepared to surrender to the Indian Army. Sam responded on December 15. He promised safety and respect to all military and paramilitary personnel and to West Pakistani civilians in accordance with Geneva Conventions. The wounded would be taken care of and the dead buried with dignity. There would be no reprisals by the Indian Army. As a measure of good faith he would call on his eastern army commander to ceasefire from 5.00 pm and would expect Gen. Rao Farman Ali to issue orders to the Pakistan Army to cease hostilities. Sam warned, as much as he abhorred unnecessary loss of life, any breach of this agreement would force him to resume the offensive with rigour.

The guns went silent at 5.00 pm on December 15 although sporadic fighting continued till the message filtered down to lower headquarters. At 4.30 pm on December 16, at Dacca's Ramna Race Course, Lt Gen. Amir Abdullah Khan Niazi signed the Instrument of Surrender and handed over his pistol, lanyard and badges of rank to Lt Gen. Jagjit Singh Aurora, GOC-in-C Eastern Command, thereby placing Pakistan's eastern army under the command of the Indian Army and bringing the war to an end with the unconditional surrender of 92,000 officers and men.

Mrs Gandhi wanted Sam to take the surrender but he refused to steal a march on the eastern army commander, saying he would have proudly done so if the entire Pakistan Army had surrendered. Prior to the surrender a senior staff officer from Eastern Command was required to go to Dacca to ensure all arrangements were in place. Sam deputed Maj. Gen. Jacob, Chief of Staff, Eastern Command. When the Ministry of Defence got to know this, it expressed concern that a Jewish officer had been appointed to make arrangements for surrender by a Muslim army. The

*Sam's strategy worked ... Lt Gen. A.A.K. Niazi, commander of the Pakistani forces in East Pakistan, was prepared to surrender to the Indian Army*

**PRIME MINISTER**

No.314-PMH/71

New Delhi
December 22, 1971

Dear General Manekshaw,

The last days have given proof of the people's admiration and appreciation of the magnificent achievement of our Armed Forces in safeguarding our territorial integrity and upholding our national values.

I know how heavy has been your burden and how constant have been the pressures upon you, as Chief of the Army Staff and also as Chairman of the Chiefs of Staff Committee. The coordination between the three Services, so impressively demonstrated during the campaign, owes much to your brilliant leadership. I particularly valued your cooperation, your clear-headed counsel and unfailing good cheer throughout this crisis.

I should like to express the gratitude of the Government and the people of India to you and to your officers and men.

With kindes regards,

Yours sincerely,

(Indira Gandhi)

General S.H.F.J. Manekshaw,
Chief of the Army Staff,
New Delhi.

---

DO No 70012/4/COAS

24    December 1971

I am in receipt of your DO letter No 314-PMH/71 of 22 Dec 71, for which I thank you.

It was gracious of you to have been so generous with your praise and I am most appreciative. I shall convey your sentiments to the Army.

May I also thank you for the trust and confidence you placed in me and for giving me my head throughout.

With my warm personal regards,

Mrs INDIRA GANDHI
Prime Minister
NEW DELHI.

---

LEFT:
Indira Gandhi's letter congratulating Sam

RIGHT:
Sam's response to the prime minister
Courtesy: The Manekshaw family

government was concerned how this would be viewed by Muslim nations friendly to India. Sam was outraged and asked why the government had been silent for thirty years when Jake (Jacob) had risked his life for the nation. The army was above religion, caste or creed and in any case it was too late, for Jake was on his way. After putting down the phone, Sam called Jake to let him know what had transpired. Understandably, Jake became sentimental and threatened to resign. For Sam this was the last straw, 'Jake, now don't try that one on me, for if you put in your papers, I will accept them.' Jacob was a very capable officer and the arrangements were perfect.

During the war Sam had acted in good faith but he had undoubtedly ruffled feathers. Air Chief Marshal P.C. Lal writes in his autobiography, *My Years with the IAF* (1986), that he felt slighted by the army chief's 'public announcements and declarations that implied that he, and he alone, was responsible for whatever had been achieved.' The last straw came on December 14 when he said that he would 'order *his* Air Force' to take action. While P.C. Lal does attribute Sam's strong statements to 'a time of great stress', or a 'loose expression employed to intimidate the enemy', his grandstanding was a major irritant.[5]

Sam was very correct when it came to keeping the government informed. Each morning at

---

5 Air Chief Marshal Pratap Chandra Lal, *My Years with the IAF* (Lancers International, 1986)

8.30 am the prime minister and the defence minister were briefed by all the three service chiefs in the 'war room' established in South Block. They would report gains, losses and casualty figures of the past twenty-four hours and plans for the next twenty-four. Maj. Gen. M.N. Batra would brief the world press each evening, in time for them to meet publication deadlines. The information would be in the public domain by the following morning.

During the war, Sam's old battalion, 4/12 FFR (now 6 FFR of the Pakistan Army), captured a portion of the bund near Fazilka in Indian Punjab. Repeated efforts by our troops to dislodge them failed. After every unsuccessful bid, the loudspeaker would triumphantly blare forth from behind the captured bund, *'Ham Sam Sahib ki paltan se hain aur kabhi piche nahin hatenge.'* (We are from Sam Sahib's battalion and will never withdraw.) What a compliment to his leadership from his old battalion![6] Sam could barely conceal his pride when briefings referred to 'the impregnable 6 FFR'. When the Pakistan government conferred the Nishan-e-Haider, the highest gallantry award, on Maj. Shabbir Sharif of 6 FFR, Sam took great pride in this achievement by 'his battalion officer' and wrote about it to his old British CO.[7]

Although the Indian Army was euphoric about victory, there was an element of disappointment with the declaration of ceasefire. Commanders wanted to capture objectives that were well within reach, but the government had decided to call a halt. Mrs Gandhi, during her tour of the US and Europe, had stressed that India had no 'hidden agenda' of territorial gain. Opponents of this point of view continue to claim that India should have been more politically astute, leveraged its ascendent position, dealt a decisive blow to Pakistan on the western front and settled all outstanding issues from 1947, including Kashmir. But this was nothing new; the army's gains are always squandered through political paralysis.

On the day Dacca fell Mrs Gandhi could barely contain her excitement. She ran up the stairs of Parliament House and interrupted proceedings to announce victory. Pakistan had been trounced in less than two weeks against a projected time frame of four to six weeks. The house exploded with jubilation; it was India's finest hour. ◆

*During the war Sam had acted in good faith but he had undoubtedly ruffled feathers*

---

6 Courtesy: Maj. Gen. K.S. Bajwa.
7 Courtesy: 'Sam Manekshaw' by Hamid Hussain, South Asia Contact Group.

The investiture ceremony
at the Ashoka Hall of
Rashtrapati Bhavan

FACING PAGE:
Army Day Parade, January
15, 1973

Courtesy: 58 Gorkha Training Centre

# The Finest Hour

With India's decisive victory, the army chief became a cause célèbre. In his office a framed copy of the surrender document was displayed with pride. The document had been drafted by him, and cleared by the defence secretary, K.B. Lal, and by the secretary to the prime minister, P.N. Haksar. Sam dictated the contents on phone to Headquarters Eastern Command and told them to get four originals: one each for the records at Army Headquarters and Eastern Command, one for Gen. Niazi and one for his office. This was his treasured memento.

The country was euphoric. The Indian Army had vindicated itself and the demons of the 1962 Chinese debacle had been exorcised. The groundswell of public appreciation and gratitude made the halo of victory shine bright for all the men and women in uniform. With units still in forward locations, Army Headquarters recommended that the Republic Day[1] parade be cancelled, but Mrs Gandhi wanted the pageant. There was a victory to celebrate and there were tributes to pay. The Amar Jawan Jyoti, a simple war memorial with a helmet on an inverted rifle, was erected at short notice by the CPWD under the canopy of India Gate. On January 26, 1972, before the

---

1 India's Republic Day, January 26, is celebrated with a military parade and a pageant to showcase the cultural diversity of the country.

<u>INSTRUMENT OF SURRENDER SIGNED AT DACCA AT *1631* HOURS (IST)</u>

<u>ON 16 DEC 1971</u>

The PAKISTAN Eastern Command agree to surrender all PAKISTAN
Armed Forces in BANGLA DESH to Lieutenant-General JAGJIT SINGH AURORA,
General Officer Commanding in Chief of the Indian and BANGLA DESH forces
in the Eastern Theatre.  This surrender includes all PAKISTAN land, air
and naval forces as also all para-military forces and civil armed forces.
The forces will lay down their arms and surrender at the places where
they are currently located to the nearest regular troops under the
command of Lieutenant-General JAGJIT SINGH AURORA.

The PAKISTAN Eastern Command shall come under the orders of
Lieutenant-General JAGJIT SINGH AURORA as soon as this instrument has
been signed.  Disobedience of orders will be regarded as a breach of
the surrender terms and will be dealt with in accordance with the
accepted laws and usages of war.  The decision of Lieutenant-General
JAGJIT SINGH AURORA will be final, should any doubt arise as to the
meaning or interpretation of the surrender terms.

Lieutenant-General JAGJIT SINGH AURORA gives a solemn assurance
that personnel who surrender shall be treated with dignity and respect
that soldiers are entitled to in accordance with the provisions of the
GENEVA Convention and guarantees the safety and well-being of all
PAKISTAN military and para-military forces who surrender.  Protection
will be provided to foreign nationals, ethnic minorities and personnel
of WEST PAKISTAN origin by the forces under the command of Lieutenant-
General JAGJIT SINGH AURORA.


(JAGJIT SINGH AURORA)
Lieutenant-General
General Officer Commanding in Chief
Indian and BANGLA DESH Forces in the
Eastern Theatre

16 December 1971.

(AMIR ABDULLAH KHAN NIAZI)
Lieutenant-General
Martial Law Administrator Zone B and
Commander Eastern Command (PAKISTAN)

16 December 1971.

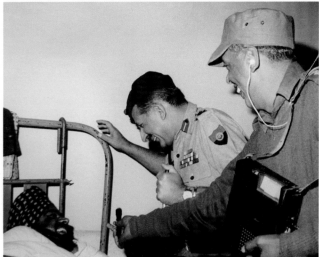

commencement of the parade, the prime minister drove down Rajpath in an open jeep, followed by the three service chiefs, to pay homage to the fallen. A scaled-down version of the parade followed. Contingents marched down Rajpath in battle fatigues rather than ceremonial uniforms. The government instituted five new medals for the armed forces, one for all personnel who were on the strength of their organisation on December 3, 1971, the day the war commenced; one each for those who had fought in the eastern and/or western theatres of war; one to celebrate twenty-five years of Independence; and a wound medal. Sam ensured that the last of these would be awarded to personnel wounded in operations after 1947, thereby excluding himself from receiving another medal for his WWII injuries. This was the standard of integrity that he set for himself and expected of his officers.

But the army chief could hardly rest on his laurels. While celebrations continued and accolades continued to pour in, Sam visited military hospitals, providing succour to the grievously wounded and disabled and boosting the morale of overstretched hospital staff. A wounded and traumatised Pakistani soldier opened up to him and confided his humiliation at being taken prisoner, blaming his senior officers for the debacle. Sam consoled the man and commended his bravery, saying he should take comfort from the fact that he had fought well.

Families of the fallen needed attention. The government announced that war widows would continue to receive their husbands' full salaries till their husband's date of superannuation, and two-thirds thereafter as pension. Those who were educated were given government jobs, and scholarships were awarded to their children. The Indian Railways stepped up to the plate and introduced concessional fares for gallantry award winners and bereaved families, for life.

Sam directed his military secretary (MS), Maj. Gen. A.N. Mathur (Corps of Signals), to speak to each wounded officer and ensure he was posted to a station of his choice during the period of convalescence. Among those grievously wounded was Maj. (later Maj. Gen.) Ian Cardozo of 4/5 GR. While on night patrol in Sylhet, in East Pakistan, Ian had stepped on a landmine that shattered his lower left leg. The regimental medical officer could not operate on him as

**LEFT:**
Gifting a sewing machine to a war widow

**RIGHT:**
With a wounded soldier
Courtesy: 58 Gorkha Training Centre

**FACING PAGE:**
The Surrender Document
Courtesy: The United Service Institution of India, New Delhi

*Sam visited military hospitals, providing succour ... boosting the morale of overstretched hospital staff*

At the hospital with the
wounded
Courtesy: The Manekshaw family

*The army
chief was
unhappy with
the practice of
downgrading
battle
casualties to
'low medical
category' and
denying them
command
appointments*

enemy shelling had destroyed all surgical instruments and stocks of morphine and antibiotics. In excruciating agony, Ian pleaded with his orderly to cut off the mangled limb with his khukri. When the Gorkha lost his nerve Ian grabbed the khukri, slashed off his leg below the knee and ordered his orderly to bury the stump. The next day he was operated on by a Pakistani medical officer and evacuated to the Artificial Limb Centre in Pune to be fitted with a prosthesis. He was on medical leave, convalescing, when the MS called and asked him for his choice of posting. Ian opted for Bombay, but when his posting order arrived he found he'd been posted to MS Branch, Army Headquarters, Delhi. Disappointed, he sought an interview with the MS. The army chief was unhappy with the practice of downgrading battle casualties to 'low medical category' and denying them command appointments. He wanted the current practice to be replaced with a just alternative whereby officers who overcame their disability would not be denied command. Ian had been handpicked to make this happen. Many hurdles had to be crossed because of an entrenched mindset, but his persistence paid off and the new policy was finally implemented in 1978, after Sam retired. Ian got to command his battalion, an infantry brigade and an infantry division. Sam's sense of fairness had been vindicated.

Apart from taking care of his own, there were 92,000 POWs that demanded the army chief's attention. Maj. Gen. S.K. Sinha, deputy AG, was in charge of the internment camps. The prisoners were housed in army barracks and provided with all the amenities that Indian soldiers were entitled to, while displaced Indian soldiers lived in tents. The International Red Cross and the

**Visiting the Artificial Limb Centre in Pune. Alongside is the Director General of Medical Services and behind him, third from right, is General G.G. Bewoor, Southern Army Commander**
Courtesy: 58 Gorkha Training Centre

international press were given free access to the POW camps for the world to see that the Indian Army had the integrity and moral standing of a superior force and treated prisoners above and beyond the provisions of the Geneva Convention. This has been covered in greater detail in the Foreword by Gen. Sinha.

A month after the war ended Sam was summoned by Mrs Gandhi to her residence at 1 Safdarjung Road and handed a file compiled by RAW[2] that documented transgressions by a handful of senior Indian Army officers in East Pakistan. The list was comprehensive and included room numbers at the Dacca Intercontinental Hotel where women had been procured for entertainment. Sam was outraged but told the prime minister that public disclosure would be counterproductive and besmirch the reputation of the entire army for the lapses of a few. He assured her that he would take care of each defaulter in good time. The axe fell silently but surely.

One of the generals on the list was an excellent field commander. A few months after the war he was shortlisted by the MS to become adjutant general. When the file reached the chief's office, Sam returned it with the comment, 'Over my dead body! The adjutant general is the custodian of discipline in the Indian Army. If this officer becomes adjutant general, this chief will have sleepless nights.' Career sealed, the officer retired.

---

2 Research and Analysis Wing is the external intelligence agency of India.

DO No 70012/10/COAS                              17    Dec 71

I send you my warmest felicitations
and heartiest congratulations on this great
day when your Country has been liberated
by the combined effort of your forces and
the Armed Forces under my command. You
will remember, Sir, that I had given you my
solemn assurance that I would leave no stone
unturned to help you in the deliverance of
your Country.   I am grateful to the Almighty
that He has made it possible for me to keep
my word to you.

I wish you great joy and will take the
first opportunity, as soon as I am free from
my preoccupations in the West, to come
personally to congratulate you and offer my
felicitations.

With my warm regards and high
esteem,

His Excellency Syed NAZRUL ISLAM
Acting President
People's Republic of BANGLADESH
DACCA

Sam's letter to Syed Nazrul Islam, Acting President, Bangladesh
Courtesy: The Manekshaw family

From: His Excellency Syed Nazrul Islam,
      Acting President of the Government
      of the People's Republic of
      Bangladesh.

**President's Secretariat**

Mujibnagar.

D. O.  No.PS/XVI/322

Dated, 20th December, 1971

My dear General,

Thank you very much indeed for your kind letter of felici-
tation. Really, you have redeemed your pledge. In less than a
fortnight you have clinched the issue. The enemy was out-fought,
out-manoeuvred and out-witted. This was a masterstroke of military
strategy —— immense in daring and tremendous in victory. The
people of Bangladesh will remember with a sense of ever-lasting
gratitude the services rendered by the allied forces under your
able command. For this resounding success, on behalf of my people,
my Cabinet members as well as my own behalf I offer you my hearties
congratulations and through you to all the Officers, NCOs and
members of other rank under your command.

At this moment of happiness I remember with deep sense of
sorrow those valiant officers and soldiers who have laid down their
lives for the cause of Bangladesh. Kindly convey to the members of
the bereaved families my sincerest sympathy for the great loss that
they have sustained. May the souls of the martyrs rest in eternal
peace.

I am looking forward to the day on which I shall have the
pleasure to receive you in our midst. I am sure that you will keep
your this pledge as well.

With kindest regards,

Yours sincerely,

(Syed Nazrul Islam)

General SHFJ Manekshaw, M.C.
Chief of the Army Staff.

**Reply from Syed Nazrul Islam, Acting President, Bangladesh**
Courtesy: The Manekshaw family

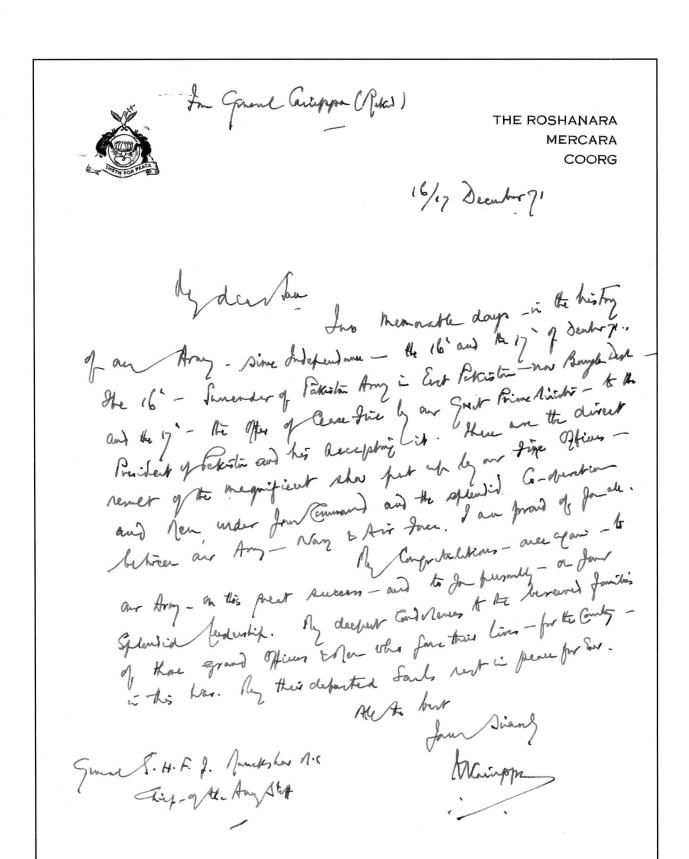

For General Cariappa (Retd)

THE ROSHANARA
MERCARA
COORG

16/17 December 71

My dear Sam

Two memorable days — in the history of our Army — since Independence — the 16th and the 17th of December 71. The 16th — Surrender of Pakistan Army in East Pakistan — now Bangla Desh — and the 17th — the offer of Cease Fire by our Great Prime Minister — to the President of Pakistan and his accepting it. These are the direct result of the magnificent show put up by our fine Officers — and Men, under your Command and the splendid Co-operation between our Army — Navy & Air Force. I am proud of you all. My Congratulations — once again — to our Army — on this great success — and to you personally — on your splendid leadership. My deepest Condolences to the bereaved families of those gallant Officers & Men who gave their lives — for the Country — in this War. May their departed Souls rest in peace for ever.

All the best

Yours Sincerely

K M Cariappa

General S.H.F.J. Manekshaw MC
Chief of the Army Staff

Letter from General Cariappa congratulating Sam for the 1971 victory
Courtesy: The Manekshaw family

I have just this minute received your letter of 17 Dec 71 sending your congratulations on the two memorable days in the history of our Army since Independence. You are very kind.

This war has been pretty "bloody". We have suffered heavy casualties both in dead and wounded and considerable losses in equipment. Our enemy has fared much worse both regarding human as well as material attrition and now we have the problem of nearly 95,000 Prisoners of War. I am sure you will support me in my belief and orders that all those men as also their families who are now our prisoners, shall be treated with the utmost courtesy and dignity - which I think, is the birth-right of any soldier. Many in this Country are critical of this measure but I cannot believe that any other action would be right.

Our officers and men have fought valiantly and our erstwhile enemy has also shown great courage. Should you be coming North, it would do the men a great deal of good were you to visit them in the various hospitals where they are now being treated. Silloo spends from early morning to late at night every spare moment of her time at the Hospital and has organised much to make the injured and the maimed feel more comfortable.

With my warm personal regards and thank you once again for writing.

General KM CARIAPPA (Retd)
The Roshanara
MERCARA
COORG.

Sam's response to General Cariappa
Courtesy: The Manekshaw family

17 December 1971

General S.H.F.J. Manekshaw
Chief of the Army Staff
Army Headquarters
New Delhi


Dear General Manekshaw:

As one professional soldier to another, please accept my
heartiest congratulations of the smashing victory of the Indian
Army. I believe military history will show the campaign in
Bangla Desh to be one of the best led and best executed of
modern times.

I am very sorry that the relations of our two countries have
deteriorated so badly. I sincerely hope that the future will
allow us to build on past foundations and keep a meaningful
dialogue between our professional forces.

Once again, congratulations to the Indian Army and its
outstanding leaders.

Sincerely,

JOHN A. HOEFLING
Brigadier General, U.S. Army
Defense Supply Representative

Letter from Brigadier General Hoefling of the US Army
Courtesy: The Manekshaw family

EMBASSY OF THE UNITED STATES OF AMERICA
NEW DELHI

December 20, 1971

PERSONAL AND CONFIDENTIAL

Dear Sam:

I want to extend to you my personal congratulations for the magnificent performance of your army during the recent difficult days. From all accounts, your forces have acquitted themselves in a manner which merits their being described as outstandingly competent professionals.

Perhaps even more impressive to me has been the opportunity to see the text of the various messages which you exchanged with the Commander of the Pakistan army in the East. The magnanimity which you have shown in the hour of victory towards a force whose conduct has left much to be desired, as we all know, has earned my lasting admiration.

With warmest personal regards.

Very sincerely yours,

Kenneth B. Keating

General S. H. F. J. Manekshaw, M. C.
Chief of Army Staff
Ministry of Defence
New Delhi

Letter from Kenneth Keating, US Ambassador
Courtesy: The Manekshaw family

From: Air Chief Marshal P C Lal D F C

AIR HEADQUARTERS
NEW DELHI

24th December, 1971

*My dear Sam,*

Many thanks for your appreciation of the work done by the Air Force in the recent hostilities.

I am glad that our arrangements for the support of the Army worked out reasonably well. For my part, I would like to say that the Army Commanders understood the capabilities and limitations of the Air Force and used it to good effect.

Thanks are due to you also for the manner in which you ran the affairs of the Chiefs of Staff Committee. Your broad outlook and ready understanding of fast changing situations contributed greatly to the success of our operations.

On behalf of the Air Force and on my own behalf, I congratulate you for your personal leadership, and for the Army's fine performance.

*With all good wishes*
*Yours sincerely*
*Pratap*

General S. H. F. J. Manekshaw, MC.,
Chief of the Army Staff,
Army Headquarters,
NEW DELHI - 11.

Letter from Air Chief Marshal P.C. Lal
Courtesy: The Manekshaw family

ADMIRAL S. M. NANDA, PVSM
CHIEF OF THE NAVAL STAFF

NAVAL HEADQUARTERS
NEW DELHI - 11

28th December, 1971.

My dear Sam,

On behalf of myself and the Navy, I would like to thank you for your kind words of praise and encouragement.

We in the Navy feel proud that we were shoulder to shoulder with our Army and Air Force in this struggle and were able to participate effectively in these momentous events. It has given us a full measure of confidence in ourselves and an even better appreciation of the powerful capabilities of our sister Services. Undoubtedly also the liberation of BANGLA DESH will remain as a brilliant chapter in the annals of military history with the classic advances made by our Army in such record time.

Much has been said, and rightly so, about the well co-ordinated efforts and planning of the three Services. Undoubtedly, we have come a long way in this regard and your Chairmanship of the Chiefs of Staff has contributed in no small measure to this success.

I would be grateful if my appreciation could be conveyed to your officers and men.

With kind regards.

Yours sincerely,

S.M. Nanda.

*File on as personal file*

*Bro.*

*QA.   28/12/71*

*1376*

General S.H.F.J. MANEKSHAW, M.C.,
Chief of the Army Staff,
Army Headquarters,
NEW DELHI-11.

Letter from Admiral S.M. Nanda, Chief of the Naval Staff
Courtesy: The Manekshaw family

At Lahore airport with
General Tikka Khan
Courtesy: 58 Gorkha Training Centre

Another defaulter on RAW's list had been endorsed by the defence minister for promotion to army commander. Sam wrote to Mrs Gandhi questioning the minister's decision, 'As I told you this morning, I think the Defence Minister's views could be discounted as he neither had knowledge, nor objectivity with regard to these promotions … You and I know all about [the officer]: although professionally he is capable, morally he is not fit to be an officer, leave alone an Army Commander … not only did he steal, [and] keep women, but he has lied … If he were to be made an Army Commander the whole Army would feel let down … I think you will agree with me that he can never be made an Army Commander.'[3] The prime minister agreed and that put paid to the career of another officer who had wilfully disobeyed his orders.

After the war, Sam visited Eastern Command to congratulate officers on their performance. At the Calcutta airport instead of the Austin Sheerline was a Mercedes Benz looted from East Pakistan, with four stars and his flag. He walked right past it and got into an ordinary Indian Ambassador car and, without his star plate or flag, told the driver to take him to his destination. The message rang out loud and clear.

Prior to relinquishing office, as part of his farewell rounds, Sam was scheduled to visit a formation in Eastern Command. After the dates were confirmed, I received a call from the formation commander, inviting the chief to dinner at his home. Sam told me to regret the invitation for the officer had been on the take, and his name had figured prominently on RAW's list. The next day the commander called again, this time to invite Sam to cocktails. Once again I was told to regret the invitation, 'By the way, Beroze, you don't need to give him a reason.' When the commander persisted for the third time, Sam said to me, 'Just tell him I'm dead. Also tell him not to come to the airport to receive me.' Sam stayed under his own arrangements, attended cocktails at the Officers' Mess to compliment his officers on their brilliant performance and returned to Delhi the next day. He kept the formation commander at arm's length all evening.

By March 1972 the Indian Army had handed over the administration of Bangladesh to civil authorities and was back in its barracks. Sam had reached the age of superannuation and was due

---

3 Source: The Manekshaw family letters.

to retire on April 3, 1972. He wrote to the prime minister to relieve him of his duties, but she was not willing to let him go without settling matters relating to territories captured during the war and the settlement of the issue of 92,000 POWs. On April 1, through a presidential decree Sam was asked to continue in office. 'The President hereby orders that Gen S.H.F.J. Manekshaw shall continue to be Chief of the Army Staff at the pleasure of the President.' This was a second extension of service received during his career.

In March 1972 I returned to Delhi with my battalion from the op location. Shubhi had been nominated to attend the Staff College in the UK and in July 1972 I returned to work for Sam. In late June 1972 the prime ministers Indira Gandhi and Zulfikar Ali Bhutto met in Simla to wrap up outstanding issues related to the war and on July 2, 1972 the Simla Accord was signed. The prime ministers agreed that both sides would return all territories captured along the international border[4] during the war except in J&K, where the respective armies would negotiate the delineation of the border. According to the terms of the Simla Agreement, the 'Cease Fire Line' in J&K that Sam had helped draw in 1947 when he was DMO, would henceforth be known as the 'Line of Control' (LOC), giving it greater legitimacy. Unfortunately, India once again squandered its position of ascendency by not getting a formal sign-off by Bhutto to recognise this as an international border. Nor did we seek a permanent solution to the Kashmir issue. The only marginal gain of the LOC was that the role of the UN observers in J&K became redundant and India asked for their withdrawal.

The delineation in J&K proceeded smoothly with one exception. The village of Thako Chak in Jammu district that held strategic value for India had been captured by Pakistan. India sought its return on the grounds that it lay along the international border that ran along Pakistan's Punjab state while Pakistan claimed that it lay on the LOC.[5] On November 28, 1972 we were scheduled

TOP:
**Bound for Lahore with two Pakistani POW air force officers being repatriated as a gesture of goodwill**

ABOVE:
**Being seen off by General Tikka Khan at Lahore airport**
Courtesy: 58 Gorkha Training Centre

4 The international boundary stretches from the Rann of Kutch upto Punjab. The border in J&K is not recognised as an international boundary but as the Line of Control (LOC).

5 Source: *India's Wars Since Independence* (2010), by Maj. Gen. Sukhwant Singh, AVSM.

Talks in progress at Corps
HQ, Lahore. To the left of
Sam is Major General
Inder Gill

Courtesy: 58 Gorkha Training Centre

to leave for Tehran on an official visit at the invitation of the Shah. Our luggage had reached the airport when we received instructions from the prime minister's office to abort the visit. Instead, the next morning we flew to Lahore accompanied by the DMO, Maj. Gen. Inderjit Singh Gill, his staff officer, and the chief's MA, Lt Col. Depinder Singh. The passenger manifest included two Pakistani POW Air Force officers released as a gesture of goodwill by the Indian government.

We were received at Lahore airport by Gen. Tikka Khan, Pakistan's army chief, his son and aide, Capt. Khalid Khan, and senior Pakistan Army officers. The atmosphere was tense and frosty. Sam knew Tikka from the IMA where he was a course junior. Both were boxers in the same weight category and during an annual boxing tournament they were pitted against each other. They both boxed well and up until the last minute their scores were on par. With a few seconds to go Tikka lowered his guard to wipe his glove when Sam delivered a stinging right hook that knocked Tikka down.[6] By a strange quirk of fate, Sam had delivered a second knockout punch in the 1971 war. Sam joked and tried to put Tikka at ease, but though his humour did thaw some of the frost, tension was palpable and lurking round the corner.

The talks were held at Corps HQ followed by lunch at the residence of the governor of Punjab, Ghulam Mustafa Khar. The Thako Chak impasse was not easy to resolve. After spinning its wheels the delegation returned to Delhi that evening without success. Eight days later, on December 7, 1972, we again flew to Lahore for talks. A few minutes into the flight Sam asked Inder Gill for the map of Thako Chak. The DMO turned to his staff officer who rummaged

*By a strange
quirk of fate,
Sam had
delivered
a second
knockout
punch in
the 1971 war*

---

6 Related by Brig. Vivek Sapatnekar (Parachute Regiment).

through his briefcase and broke into cold sweat. There were maps of the entire western border with Pakistan except Thako Chak! Unfazed, Gill told his staff officer to relax and turning to Sam he said, 'Sorry, Chief, you can't have the map, it's probably somewhere in my office.' Equally unperturbed, Sam replied, 'Never mind, Inder, we'll use Tikka's map *and* we will return with Thako Chak,' prophetic words indeed, for that is precisely how the dice fell.

The deadlock persisted through lunch. That afternoon Sam tabled a proposal. If Pakistan returned Thako Chak, India would abandon its claim to the two villages of Dhum and Ghilkot measuring 0.45 square miles. These villages were surrounded on three sides by Pakistan and presented a challenge to hold. Tikka agreed in principle but needed the concurrence of his prime minister. He turned to Sam and asked if he would like to speak to Mrs Gandhi. That was not necessary. The prime minister had told Sam to surrender Thako Chak if the negotiations deadlocked again, but he was determined not to give in. Eventually Pakistan conceded to India's claim and the delegation returned to Delhi after successful negotiations. On December 11, 1972 the army commanders of India and Pakistan, Lt Gen. P.S. Bhagat and Lt Gen. Abdul Hamid Khan, met at Suchetgarh and signed off on the maps that delineated the 800 km long LOC in J&K. These maps were ratified by their respective governments and with that the withdrawal of troops to pre-war positions began.

In retrospect what stands out is the distance that the Pakistan and the Indian armies have travelled since 1972. In Pakistan, the army is the power centre that crafts state policy and takes strategic decisions. In India, although the army has never displayed political ambitions, politicians and bureaucrats have ensured that its advice is seldom sought and, if offered, it is sacrificed at the altar of political expediency.

On the sidelines of this trip there were several small incidents that are worthy of mention. It was agreed that all members of the delegation would be in service dress and peak-caps. Sam, true to style, disobeyed his own instructions and wore a *mazri*[7] shirt and side-cap. At Palam airport Gill sauntered up to him and asked why he disobeyed his own orders and got a gleeful response, 'Inder, because *I* am Chief!' Sam and Gill were two of a kind—bold, outspoken and honest.

भारत के राष्ट्रपति का संयुक्त सचिव,
राष्ट्रपति भवन,
JOINT SECRETARY TO THE PRESIDENT OF INDIA,
RASHTRAPATI BHAVAN,
NEW DELHI-110004.
नई दिल्ली-110004.

January 1, 1973.

Dear General Manekshaw,

The President will be pleased to confer the insignia of the rank of Field Marshal of the Indian Army on you at a special ceremony to be held at 11.00 a.m. on Tuesday, January 2, 1973, at the Ashoka Hall, Rashtrapati Bhavan. I am desired by the President to request you to be present on the occasion and receive the insignia.

The President will be pleased if Shrimati Manekshaw will also attend the ceremony.

Please accept my sincere congratulations.

With kind regards,

Yours sincerely,

(P. N. Krishna Mani)

General S. H F. J. Manekshaw, M.C.,
Chief of the Army Staff,
"Army House",
4, King George's Avenue,
New Delhi.

Letter from the government informing the army chief of the decision to confer on him the rank of field marshal
Courtesy: The Manekshaw family

---

7 A *mazri* shirt is made of light grey cots wool material and is the official uniform of the Assam Rifles, a paramilitary force.

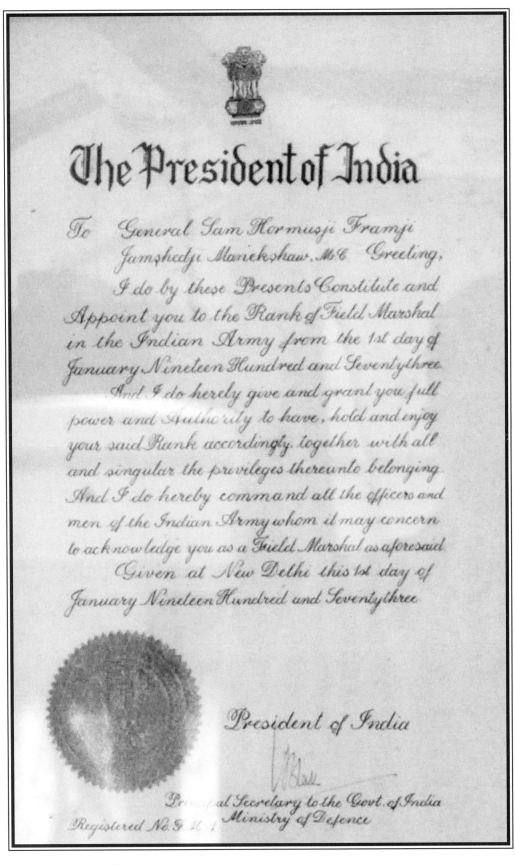

**Citation for rank of Field Marshal**
Courtesy: 58 Gorkha Training Centre

# भारत का राष्ट्रपति

जनरल सैम हॉर्मुसजी फ्रामजी जमशेदजी
मानेकशा, रम.सी.        को स्वस्तिवचन,

मैं इन उपहारों द्वारा आपको भारतीय थल सेना में
फील्ड मार्शल  के रैंक में १९७३ के जनवरी मास के पहले
दिवस से प्रतिष्ठित और नियुक्त करता हूं ।

रवम् तदनुसार मैं आपको अपने उक्त रैंक को उससे
संलग्न समस्त और विशेष अधिकारों सहित ग्रहण, धारण
और उपभोग करने की पूर्ण शक्ति और प्राधिकार रततं द्वारा
प्रदान और स्वीकृत करता हूं । तथा मैं भारतीय थल सेना
के समस्त पदधारियों और व्यक्तियों को जिनका भी वास्ता
हो, आदेश देता हूं कि वे आपको उपर्युक्त रूप में फील्ड मार्शल
स्वीकार करें ।

सन् १९७३ के जनवरी मास के आज पहले दिवस
को नई दिल्ली में प्रदत्त ।

भारत का राष्ट्रपति

रक्षा मंत्रालय में भारत सरकार का,
प्रमुख सचिव

पंजीयन संख्या रफ...

**Citation for rank of Field Marshal**
Courtesy: 58 Gorkha Training Centre

TOP:
Tea with Vice President
G.S. Pathak, President V.V.
Giri and Prime Minister
Indira Gandhi
Courtesy: 58 Gorkha Training Centre

ABOVE:
A photo op with his ADC's
wife, Zenobia, and wives
of ADCs to the president
of India
Courtesy: Authors

During our second visit lunch was organised at the Corps Artillery Officers' Mess in Lahore. Sam was admiring the impressive trophies on display when he recognised one that belonged to his old battalion, 4/12 FFR. He could not restrain himself from asking what it was doing in an artillery mess. A Pakistani officer acknowledged that he was indeed right; it had been borrowed from the battalion for the special occasion.

Mrs Gandhi was seriously considering appointing Sam Chief of Defence Staff (CDS)[8] on Republic Day in 1972 but the move was opposed by Congress politicians led by Defence Minister Jagjivan Ram and by Air Chief Marshal P.C. Lal. The proposal was dropped and still eludes the services today, forty-two years later. But the prime minister continued to pursue Sam's promotion to the rank of field marshal. Till September 1972 it seemed unlikely this would ever come to pass. In fact, the defence minister, responding to reporters in Madras (now Chennai), said that he doubted if India would ever have a field marshal. Sam was paying the price for bypassing the minister.

In December the defence secretary called Sam seeking his approval to the order of precedence that would be established if he were to be made field marshal. Sam had been turned off by the petty fogging which had persisted for months. That evening he lost his shirt and curtly replied that he had not asked to be promoted and he would not nickel and dime with the government. Refusing to entertain any more discussion on the issue, he hung up the phone. On December 31 around 7.00 pm the defence secretary called Army House again. The government had decided to promote Sam to the rank of field marshal. The details of his entitlements were yet to be worked out, but the official announcement was to be made on the 9.00 pm prime time bulletin on All India Radio. Silloo called the cottage and asked Zenobia and me to hurry over as there was good news to share. Sherry and Maja and the immediate family were informed. As the clock inched forward, the four of us settled down in Sam's bedroom near the radio with our drinks to raise a toast. The Gorkhas and civilian staff trooped in, equally excited. It was the lead announcement and to hear the rank 'Field Marshal' prefixed to Sam's name was a

8 The overall commander of the Army, Navy and Air Force.

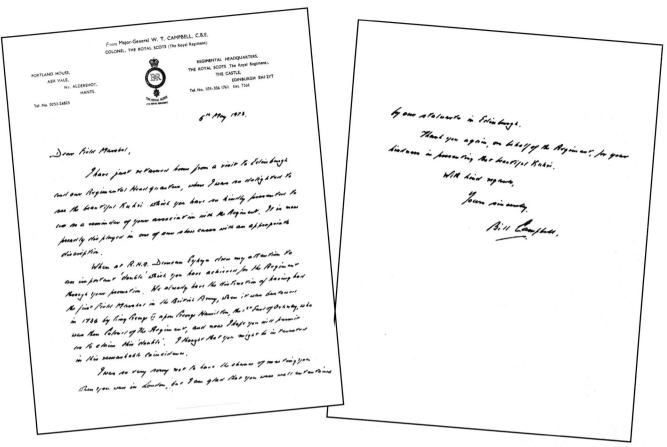

Letter from Major General
Campbell of the Royal
Scots, congratulating Sam
and staking a claim to some
of the glory
Courtesy: The Manekshaw family

surreal experience. Within minutes Army House was taken by storm. The phones rang off the hook and jubilant officers and their wives arrived to congratulate Sam and Silloo and to celebrate. The stream of well-wishers was endless.

After a while the chief turned to me and said, 'Beroze, off you go to the DSOI before Zenobia blames me for ruining your New Year's Eve.' We left for the club which was abuzz with excitement. Just before midnight Sam and Silloo arrived and were mobbed by officers and their wives. His decision to put in an appearance at the Institute was a statement of solidarity with his officers; the honour was not just his but belonged to the entire army.

According to tradition a field marshal is second only to a monarch or head of state. Just as a monarch carries the orb, a field marshal carries a baton and since regimental flags dip for a monarch or head of state, so also do they dip for a field marshal. The rank of field marshal was first introduced in the Prussian Army in the eighteenth century. In those days soldiers partook of war booty but a conquering general was excluded and as compensation he was promoted to field marshal and given a salary for life.

A special investiture ceremony was scheduled three days later. AG's branch and the chief's secretariat scrambled to get the accoutrements together. Sam needed the badges of rank of a field marshal and he needed a field marshal's baton. A week earlier, when there were indications of things to come, Bastani Brothers, military outfitters at South Block, were told to prepare cloth badges of rank of a field marshal, copying a design from the *Encyclopedia Britannica*. But these did not pass muster with Maj. Gen. S.K. Sinha who as officiating AG was in charge of the arrangements. He insisted that Sam must have metal badges. The EME[9] workshop in Delhi was tasked with the

9 Electrical and Mechanical Engineers.

*Just before midnight Sam and Silloo arrived and were mobbed by officers and their wives ... the honour was not just his but belonged to the entire army*

job. They worked round the clock and fabricated a perfect pair within twenty-four hours. Whorra Brothers at Connaught Place hastily produced an improvised baton. The actual baton arrived a couple of months later. Maj. Gen. Sinha recalls the defence ministry's intransigence. The defence secretary and the bureaucrats opposed every proposal put up by AG's branch regarding a field marshal's salary, his protocol status and his perquisites. They went to the extent of saying that a baton was not necessary since five-star generals in the US Army did not carry batons. Maj. Gen. Sinha was able to secure their consent only because the investiture ceremony was to be held forty-eight hours later, but on all other issues they insisted that a decision would be taken in due course. As we all know, the proposals went into cold storage for thirty-four years.

On January 3, 1973 in the Ashoka Hall of Rashtrapati Bhavan, Sam was pipped with his badges of rank and presented the field marshal's baton by President V.V. Giri. With that the Indian Army got its first field marshal. It was no small coincidence that in 1763 Gen. George Hamilton of the Royal Scots had been appointed the first field marshal in the British Army. The Royal Scots took great pride in Sam's promotion and called it their 'second first'. Others who celebrated Sam's recognition were Gen. Sir Roy Bucher and Field Marshal Auchinleck. Letters of congratulations poured in from around the world.

**In Delhi cantonment with Indian POWs repatriated from Pakistan**
Courtesy: 58 Gorkha Training Centre

Normanby House,
19ᵗʰ Jan 73

My dear Sam,

Thank you very much for your letter of the 6ᵗʰ Jan. We were so glad that our cable congratulating you on being promoted to Field Marshal ditto. As I have already told you, you deserve every thing that has come, or is coming, your way.

Yesterday one Mollen, of The Readers Digest, telephoned me and we spoke for over half-an-hour about you, and an article being written about you for the Digest. I will read it with great interest.

I hope Muchu will be asked to give the Nehru Memorial lecture. Will you please tell him that from me? I have been in touch with Dickie Mountbatten on the subject.

We were saddened by Rajaji's death. He was a truly great man and a kindly one too.

Maureen is telephoning along. I have heard from him & he seems cheerful, if very hard worked.

Love to both of you from Maureen and me

Yours aye,
Roy.

---

NEW DELHI

23 Jan 73

Dear Roy,

Thank you for your air letter of 19 Jan which I received this morning. You were very kind to write and as usual more than generous with your praises. I have heard from many old friends in the UK and abroad, and was most touched to get a letter from the Auk. who wrote as 'from one Field Marshal to another': it was very good of him to have written: we in the Indian Army still think very highly of him and regard him with great affection.

I see something of Muchu every now and then: we had him and his wife over for lunch about a fortnight ago and the four of us tucked into some excellent Aberdeen Angus, which my daughter Maya had sent me, frozen in one of those freezella bags. I shall tell him that you have been in touch with Dickie Mountbatten on the subject of Muchu being asked to give the Nehru Memorial lecture.

I am having a very restful time at present: relaxing in the sun and pottering about the garden: coming in Silloo's way; and drinking lashings of whisky and eating good food. It seems wonderful not to have any worries or problems after years and years of grind. Anyway, I wonder now long I shall be allowed this freedom.

.... PTO

**LEFT TO RIGHT:**
Letter from Sir Roy Bucher, and page 1 of Sam's reply to Sir Roy Bucher
Courtesy: The Manekshaw family

PERSONAL AND
CONFIDENTIAL

DO No 70012/1/COAS                                    Jan 73

Dear Prime Minister.

Last year on 3 Apr, when I had reached the age
of superannuation, I had expressed my desire to fade
away from the Army, but as many problems existed
and because of the uncertainties prevailing then, the
President was reluctant to let me go, and so I am
still continuing in office under Presidential pleasure.

Most of the immediate problems, as a consequence
of the last Conflict, now appear to have been resolved.
The Line of Control has been delineated: troops have
been withdrawn to the International Border: the shortcomings in our organisational set-up have been put
right: reorganisation of Armour, Artillery and Infantry
has commenced and will be completed shortly: deficiencies
in equipment and manpower have been made up and the
material resources expended during the War have been
recouped.  I feel, therefore, that the time has now come
for me to relinquish my office and let a younger man
take over.  If you are agreeable, perhaps I can hand over
my assignment on the 15th of this month after bidding
my officers and men farewell at the Army Day Parade.
It would also be a fit occasion for my successor to take
over from me on Army Day.  Would you please request
the President to see his way to release me.

It has been a remarkable experience working
with you, knowing how much trust and confidence you
have placed in me: I hope I never for a moment
gave you any cause to doubt either my integrity or
loyalty.  It was a pleasure working with a
Prime Minister from whom one hid nothing and with
whom one had so much rapport.  I thank you for
the confidence you have shown in me and also for
giving me my head.

I wish you and your family a very happy
New Year and may you have much joy in 1973.

Mrs INDIRA GANDHI
Prime Minister
NEW DELHI.

PERSONAL AND
CONFIDENTIAL

Sam's letter to Indira Gandhi
Courtesy: The Manekshaw family

Personal and
Confidential

PRIME MINISTER'S HOUSE
NEW DELHI

January 2, 1973.

Dear Field Marshal,

I have your letter of January 1. I appreciate
the high sense of public duty which has inspired you
to ask to be allowed to relinquish your office and let
a younger man take over from you as Chief of the Army
Staff. Accordingly I am arranging for you to hand
over your assignment on January 15 after bidding farewell
to your officers and men at the Army Day Parade.

My colleagues and I in the Government deeply
value the contribution you have made as Chief of the
Army Staff and as Chairman of the Committee of Chiefs
of Staff during the extremely critical period through
which we passed last year. The honour which Government
have conferred by promoting you to the rank of Field
Marshal is not merely a tribute to your many personal
qualities, but symbolises the valour and patriotism
of our Defence Forces as a whole.

I am glad to note that before relinquishing the
charge of your duties and responsibilities, you have
taken steps leading to the reorganisation of Armour,
Artillery and Infantry and to the making up of the
deficiencies in equipment and manpower.

With every good wish for the New Year,

Yours sincerely,

(Indira Gandhi)

Field Marshal SHFJ Manekshaw,
Chief of the Army Staff,
New Delhi.

**Indira Gandhi's response to the Army Chief**
Courtesy: The Manekshaw family

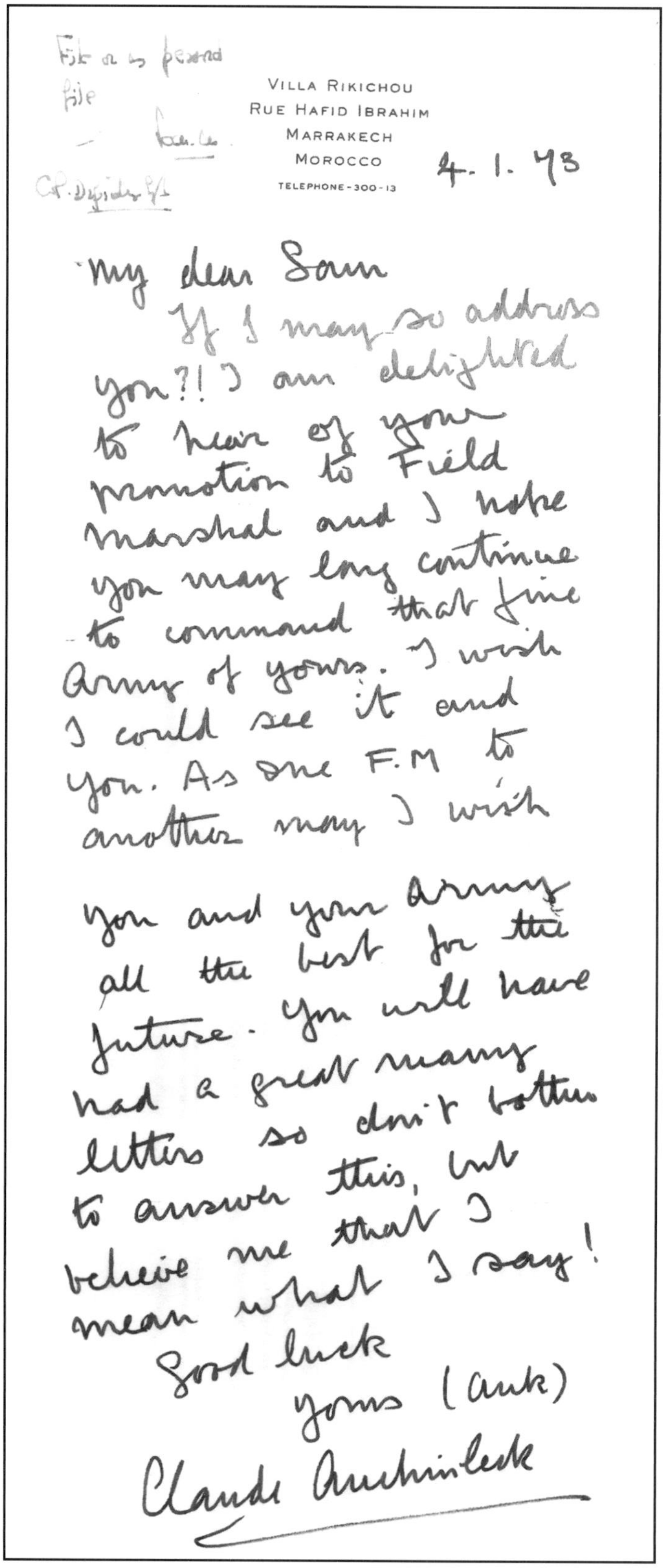

For a ... personal
file
....
Cp. Dyorder 8/1

VILLA RIKICHOU
RUE HAFID IBRAHIM
MARRAKECH
MOROCCO
TELEPHONE-300-13

4.1.73

My dear Sam
If I may so address you?! I am delighted to hear of your promotion to Field Marshal and I hope you may long continue to command that fine Army of yours. I wish I could see it and you. As one F.M to another may I wish

you and your Army all the best for the future. You will have had a great many letters so don't bother to answer this, but believe me that I mean what I say!
Good luck
Yours (Auk)
Claude Auchinleck

**Letter from Field Marshal Auchinleck**
Courtesy: The Manekshaw family

BRITISH HIGH COMMISSION
NEW DELHI

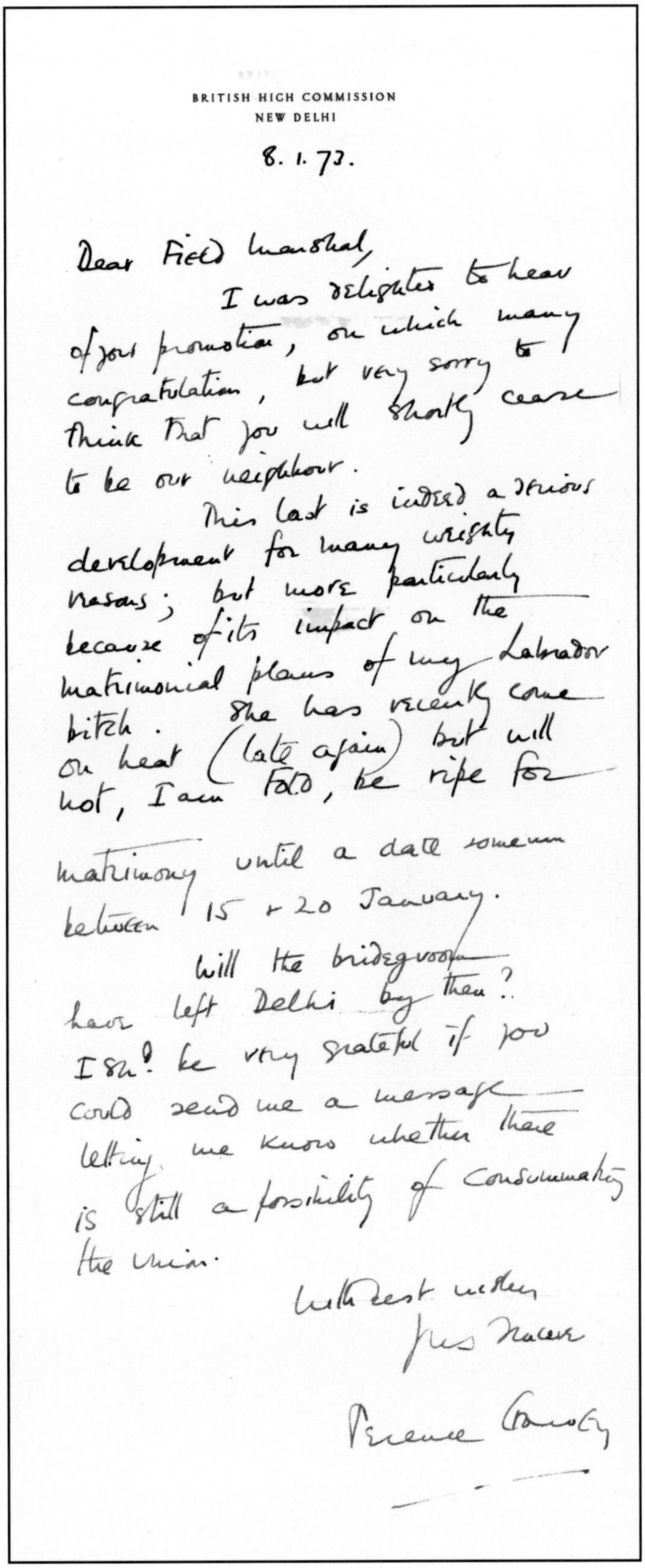

8. 1. 73.

Dear Field Marshal,

I was delighted to hear of your promotion, on which many congratulations, but very sorry to think that you will shortly cease to be our neighbour.

This last is indeed a serious development for many weighty reasons; but more particularly because of its impact on the matrimonial plans of my Labrador bitch. She has recently come on heat (late again) but will not, I am told, be ripe for matrimony until a date somewhere between 15 + 20 January.

Will the bridegroom have left Delhi by then? I sh'd be very grateful if you could send me a message letting me know whether there is still a possibility of consummating the union.

With best wishes
Yours sincerely
Terence Garvey

**British High Commissioner's primary concern**
Courtesy: The Manekshaw family

TOP:
Farewell visit to a forward
area, with Lieutenant
General Z.C. Bakshi

ABOVE:
Walking out of South Block
with his successor, General
G.G. Bewoor
Courtesy: 58 Gorkha Training Centre

In 1973 the pension of the service chiefs was Rs 1,500 a month. Since Sam was promoted to field marshal the government added a paltry Rs 100 and pegged his monthly salary at Rs 1,600 and that is where it remained with no increments and no adjustments for dearness allowance[10] until a few months before his death.

On January 1, 1973 Field Marshal Sam Manekshaw wrote to Mrs Gandhi that all follow-up actions to the 1971 war were now complete. POWs taken by India and Pakistan had been repatriated, the Thako Chak issue had been resolved, the Line of Control in J&K had been delineated and troop withdrawal had begun. He would like to hang up his boots on January 15, 1973, Army Day. This time she agreed.

Each year Army Day is celebrated with a military parade in the cantonment's parade grounds. That year the parade was a farewell to India's field marshal. For the first time regimental colours were on parade. This was a surprise for Sam. As they were walking to the saluting base he turned to Maj. Gen. Sinha and asked, 'Tell me, Sweetie, how should I respond to the salute?' Not quite sure, but not one to be stumped either, the general replied, 'By raising the baton in your right hand, Sir.' Sam accepted his advice thereby setting a new tradition in the Indian

---

10 Dearness Allowance (DA) is a Cost of Living Adjustment (COLA) to salaries and pensions to keep pace with inflation.

Army. British field marshals hold the baton in the left hand and salute with the right hand.

After the parade, Sam drove to South Block. As his cavalcade with escort jeeps and CMP outriders left the parade grounds, he brought the curtain down on an era. At the stroke of midday he handed over the office of COAS to Gen. G.G. Bewoor and went outside South Block to inspect a Guard of Honour presented by Maj. (later Lt Gen.) Rostum K. Nanavatty of 2/8 GR.

The civilian staff of Army Headquarters abandoned their desks and flocked outdoors to bid farewell to a man who had given them so much respect. With a wave to the crowd he got into the Dodge, the 'Number 2 car', leaving the Impala, the 'Number 1 car', for his successor and drove to the MES Inspection Bungalow (IB) in Delhi cantonment. With that Field Marshal Sam Hormusji Framji Jamshedji Manekshaw completed a journey that had begun on a drill square at the IMA almost four decades earlier. ◆

TOP:
Farewell Guard of Honour,
January 15, 1973

ABOVE:
Au revoir to the civilian
staff of his secretariat
Courtesy: 58 Gorkha Training Centre

STAVKA

FIELD MARSHAL
SAM MANEKSHAW

Stavka nameplate at the
entrance

FACING PAGE:
The hous[...]
Courtesy: Authors

# Stavka

The MES Inspection Bungalow in the Delhi cantonment served as a temporary residence to Sam while Stavka, his new home, named by Sherry after the country house of a Russian general, was still under construction. The volume of official mail continued, unabated, for mistakenly it was believed that he still held office since a field marshal never retires. Although I was no longer officially assigned to work for him, my services were extended to him by my CO in addition to my battalion duties. I helped him sort out the mail every day at the MES IB and with due diligence he answered every query that he could, or passed it on to the chief's secretariat for an official response.

When Silloo pronounced Stavka ready for occupation Sam left for Coonoor. Nestled in Tamil Nadu's picturesque Nilgiris or Blue Mountains, a stone's throw from the Defence Services Staff College at Wellington, it was a perfect retirement haven. A drive up Porter's Avenue from Sim's Park on the Kottagiri Road, past bungalows with quaint names like Redbrook, Fairlight, Windrose, Wildflower and Rosary, leads to Stavka. A steep climb to the top of a hill reveals a beautiful villa surrounded by terraced gardens. Sam had his work cut out for him. With his arrival

the garden took shape. Annuals, perennials and his favourite roses bordered emerald green lawns at each level. His pet peeve was that Silloo would snip off his best blooms for indoor arrangements.

The house itself is the embodiment of genteel, gracious living. An elegant porch and spacious foyer with Silloo's grand piano set the tone as you enter the villa. A large living and dining room grace the front of the house at the main level and open onto a garden with a panoramic view of lush green hills in the daytime and the twinkling lights of Wellington and the Staff College after dark. These rooms were designed for formal entertainment. A brick trellis patio on the side of the house near the dining room is ideal for 'eat outs' on balmy winter afternoons. Upstairs is the family's private living area. Sam's bedroom furnished in elegant blue and dark Mahogany connects to Silloo's, furnished in pale pink and cream. Both bedrooms open on to a terrace garden with the same view as the rooms below. At the back of the house is the family room with sunken seating around a fireplace and the informal dining area. A collage of Silloo's paintings adorn one wall of the family room and bear testimony to her talent and her keen sense of colours. An eclectic collection of curios, antiques and art pieces speaks of the style and elegance of the lady of the house. The *pièce de résistance* is a dumb waiter that conveys piping hot food from the pantry directly below. A French window opens on to the rear of the house and a rose garden. Behind the house are quarters for the Gorkhas and personal staff.

Sam settled into his new home and adjusted well to 'retired' life. He still got up at 5.30 each morning, when his orderly arrived with his *'chota hazri'*, his morning cup of tea. After spending ten minutes on his bull-worker, he'd be off to the garden to tend his plants and his tea bushes for an hour, returning indoors for breakfast with Silloo. Apart from gardening, marketing and home maintenance were his new responsibilities and, besides his dogs, he now had to apportion his time to two Jersey cows, an aviary and his poultry.

Sam became an instant icon in the Nilgiris, admired and accosted by shopkeepers, vegetable vendors and petrol pump owners as he drove around in the Sunbeam Rapier that

BELOW:
Checking his medals

BOTTOM:
Time to admire the dahlias
Courtesy: 58 Gorkha Training Centre

CLOCKWISE:

Canon at the entrance to Stavka

One of the terraced gardens with parking space to the left

The porch and the garage

The driveway

Courtesy: Authors

LEFT:
Sam's desk and his music
system on the right wall

ABOVE:
Man Bahadur and Shul
Bahadur

FACING PAGE TOP:
Informal dining area

FACING PAGE BOTTOM:
The family room
Courtesy: Authors

the family had owned since his return from the UK in 1957. True to his ethical standards, the car displayed no flag and no star plate, for Sam needed no insignia to enhance his image. Silloo, deprived of the Sunbeam that she had driven for years, was compensated with a Maruti 800.[1]

Sam and Silloo found a ready set of friends among the officers at the Staff College and among the officers who had retired and settled in the Nilgiris. They acquired new friends among the tea planters' community. Once a year they would play host to all the Gorkha officers posted in station and their wives. The house never failed to impress visitors. Sam would take his guests on a conducted tour and, with a very straight face, he would walk them through the connecting door between his bedroom and Silloo's. After enjoying their puzzled expressions for a few minutes he would then inform them that his snoring and her insomnia made this the only workable arrangement!

Life settled down to a different pace. Sam was entitled to two orderlies since a field marshal is an active soldier. And then there was Swamy for whom the Nilgiris was home. His command now stretched from the servants' quarters to the kitchen and beyond as he barked orders and expletives at the local servants in Tamil.[2] The household staff at Stavka continued to grow of

1 An indigenous, Indian car which was very popular in the 1980s and 1990s.
2 The local language of the Nilgiris which is in the state of Tamil Nadu.

**With Vice President,
TISCO, K.C. Mehra in the
steel melting shop of their
plant in Jamshedpur**
Courtesy: 58 Gorkha Training Centre

its own accord for when his orderlies went home on leave they returned with a *'kancha'*,[3] a younger brother or cousin, who was willing to provide a helping hand around the house with the hope of recruitment in the army through a letter of recommendation from the field marshal! There was enough work to keep several pairs of hands busy, but as the retinue grew in size the quarters were no longer sufficient to house them and additional ones had to be constructed. Each evening the Gorkhas, their wives and children would commandeer Sam's bedroom to watch TV. Eventually, Silloo decided it was time to add a TV room near the family room, and so the house continued to expand.

I would be remiss if I did not write about Sam's major-domo, the longest-serving Gorkha on his staff, Havildar Shul Bahadur Gurung. Shule[4] had come to Army House as a *kancha* in 1970. A few months later he was recruited as a rifleman in 2/8 GR. After serving in the battalion, he returned to Army House as Sam's orderly. Shule rose to the rank of Havildar and after his retirement returned to work for Sam on his personal staff. He was the de facto housekeeper, accountant, driver, cook (after Swamy's passing) and supervisor of household staff, all rolled into one. He was

---

3 *'Kancha'* in Nepali means 'younger brother'. In the Indian Army it is the term used for young Gorkhas who come down to India along with a brother who's a serving soldier and work in an officer's home as a civilian staff while learning the ropes. With access to good food and exercise facilities they work at joining the army, clear their recruitment exams, undergo training and return to the regiment as soldiers. Most Gorkha officers have *'kanchas'* working in their homes.

4 A colloquial form of address where the first name is used with an 'e' at the end, therefore Shul Bahadur is addressed as 'Shule' and Man Bahadur as 'Mane'.

quick to learn Tamil and often served as an interpreter! In 1999 Silloo had a special two-room cottage built behind the main house for Shule and his family. As a matter of interest, the cottage cost more than the entire house had cost twenty-five years earlier.

Sam and Silloo took personal interest in the welfare of their household staff. Doctors and nurses at the military hospital were surprised to see the field marshal driving his orderly, Man Bahadur, to the hospital five days in a row to meet his wife who was a patient. Shule was on leave, so without hesitation Sam picked up the slack, and waited patiently till Mane was ready to be driven back.

After he relinquished office Mrs Gandhi asked Sam if he would like to go as high commissioner to the UK or become governor of Maharashtra. 'The Parsis will love that,' she said. He turned down both offers, reminding her of a decision he had taken when he took over as chief. He would not compromise his independence by seeking government office. He wished to command his army without interference.

Instead Sam threw in his lot with the private sector. The Oberoi Group, Britannia Industries, Bombay Burmah Trading Corporation, Harrison Malyalam Plantations, Nagarjuna Fertilizers and Chemicals, Borneo Timber, Indian Aluminum, Escorts and several other companies appointed him as a director on their boards. He brought to the boardroom the same acumen and discipline that had been his hallmark in the Ops Room. These multiple commitments kept him away from home for the better part of each month and led Silloo to complain that she saw less of him now than when he was in the army.

Sam never let his eye off the ball when it came to ex-servicemen. Mr M.S. Oberoi, founder and chairman, East India Hotels (the Oberoi chain) and a friend of Sam's, employed retired Gorkhas to supervise the work on his farm at Chattarpur on the outskirts of Delhi. He even employed a retired bagpiper to wake him up with the lilting sound of the 'reveille' each morning! Sam was able to use his office as director on the board of several companies to secure post-retirement employment for army personnel.

Mrs Gandhi continued to consult Sam informally. While he respected her, he was disappointed when she declared a state of emergency in 1975, curtailed the freedom of the press, and threw senior opposition leaders into jail. Her decision to send tanks into the Golden Temple[5] was indefensible and lacked foresight. She had not been correctly advised, but he decided to keep his own counsel. When she invited him to be a member of the National Integration Council, he turned down the offer but continued to meet her on his frequent visits to Delhi. Her untimely demise upset him for they had worked together for a long time and he held her in high regard in spite of a few disagreements. He flew to Delhi to attend her funeral.

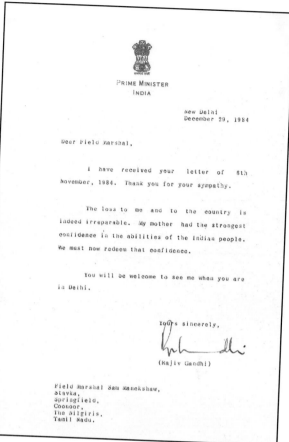

**Response from Rajiv Gandhi to Sam's letter of condolence on Indira Gandhi's demise**
Courtesy: The Manekshaw family

---

5 The most sacred temple of the Sikhs.

TOP TO BOTTOM:
**Inspecting Guard of Honour presented by the Royal Scots**

**Inspecting Guard of Honour by the British Gurkhas**
Courtesy: 58 Gorkha Training Centre

**Inspecting Guard of Honour by the Welsh Guards**
Courtesy: 2/8 Gorkha Rifles

Her son, Prime Minister Rajiv Gandhi, respected Sam and appointed him as the government's emissary to negotiate with the Shiromani Gurudwara Prabandhak Committee[6] to reduce the trust deficit between the Congress and the Sikh community after the storming of the Golden Temple and the Akal Takht.[7] Because of his standing in the Sikh community, Sam was able to bring about a modicum of rapprochement.

While staying away from most politicians Sam remained in touch with a few whom he respected. One such person was Morarji Desai, a Gandhian and a man of upright character.

On January 14, 1986 the government conferred the rank of 'honorary' field marshal on Gen. K.M. Cariappa. Sam attended the investiture ceremony at Rashtrapati Bhavan and during the reception that followed, he took Rajiv Gandhi aside and told him that the government had made a faux pas. There can be no 'honorary' field marshal. The error was quickly rectified and the next day the government withdrew the word 'honorary' from the title.

In 1973 at the invitation of Gen. Sir Michael Carver, chief of Imperial General Staff, Sam visited the UK. Officers of the Gurkha Brigade Association (GBA) of UK[8] hosted him at the 'Gurkha Pub' at Windsor. He called on Gen. Sir Roy Bucher and he visited the 2nd Battalion of the Royal Scots, in Edinburgh. Before returning, Sam hosted a dinner for all serving and retired officers of 4/12 FFR and the 8th Gorkha Rifles.

Years after relinquishing office recognition and approbation continued to pour in. In 1979 the chief of the Royal Nepalese Army invited Sam to Nepal. King Mahendra conferred on him the 'Tridhakti Patta' for his contribution to the welfare of Gorkha soldiers serving in the Indian Army. Later that year the Government of Rajasthan awarded him the 'Rana Pratap Award' for his service to the country. In 2004, Indira Gandhi Open University conferred on him the 'Honorary Doctorate of Humane Letters'. He was frequently a guest of

6 The organisation in India responsible for the upkeep of gurudwaras, Sikh places of worship.
7 Literally, the 'Seat (or the Throne) of the Timeless One'. The sanctum sanctorum.
8 The GBA is an Association of all Gurkha Regiments that belong to the British Army. At Independence there were ten Gorkha Regiments. The 2nd, 6th, 7th and 10th Regiments became part of the British Army while the 1st, 3rd, 4th, 5th, 8th and 9th Regiments remained with the Indian Army.

H.Q. & REGIMENTAL MUSEUM
OF THE FIRST OF FOOT

E R

THE ROYAL SCOTS
THE ROYAL REGIMENT

ROYAL SCOTS
( THE ROYAL REGIMENT )

NO SMOKING

At the Headquarters and
Museum of the Royal Scots
Regiment, Edinburgh
Courtesy: 58 Gorkha Training Centre

Stavka: Springfield: Coonoor

16 July 1979

        I learnt with great sadness
of your resignation: I am sorry that this
should have happened to you, you who are a
good, God fearing and decent man, whose
courage I have always admired. To think that
you have been stabbed in the back by your own
colleagues is a sad commentary on the state
of affairs existing in the political sphere
of our Country. To me Loyalty has always been
the cardinal requisite in a superior, colleague
or subordinate, but it would appear that my
Prime Minister did not get much of it. May I,
Sir, offer you my sincere sympathy and if you
do not consider it as presumption, my friendship as well. Please do not trouble to reply :
I know how busy you are. I shall consider it
a privilege to be allowed to call on you when
I am next in Delhi.
With my warm personal regards,

Mr. Morarji Desai
Prime Minister
1, Safdarjang Road
NEW DELHI

Sam's letter to Morarji Desai
Courtesy: 58 Gorkha Training Centre

सत्यमेव जयते

प्रधान मन्त्री भारत

PRIME MINISTER,
INDIA.

New Delhi,
July 20, 1979

My dear Manekshaw,

Thank you for your letter of the 16th July 1979. I appreciate the very kind sentiments expressed by you about me. This is politics but it could be much better than what it is if the people are not to lose their faith in their representatives.

I know your feelings for me and I am thankful for them. I need hardly say that I shall cherish them. You can certainly come over to meet me whenever you feel inclined to do so.

With kind regards,

Yours sincerely,

(Morarji Desai)

Field Marshal Sam Manekshaw, MC,
Stavka,
Springfield,
Coonoor.

Response from Morarji Desai
Courtesy: 58 Gorkha Training Centre

Telephone—
031- 336 1761   Ext. 7265

REGIMENTAL HEADQUARTERS,
THE ROYAL SCOTS (The Royal Regiment),
THE CASTLE,
EDINBURGH EHI 2YT

1st May 1973

My dear Field Marshall Sam,

Your wonderful surprise parcel arrived safely yesterday and we are all deeply touched by your kind and thoughtful gesture.

The beautiful Kukri will be proudly displayed by us, and will serve to do exactly what you intend it should, namely to remind us of our mutual happy association of long ago and the culmination of which is the historical achievement of your present rank. We like to think we may have had a hand in it, although a very minor one.

I rang up the Colonel of the Regiment

Major General Bill Campbell, and told him about your gift. He was both touched and delighted, and he asked me to say how sorry he was at not having an opportunity to meet you personally.

Well, Sam, best of luck to you and your wife in your retirement. I hope you will manage to drag yourselves away from your new home in the Nilgiri Hills, at sometime in the future, and come and see us again.

With kindest regards from all the old timers up here

Yours aye

Duncan

Letter from Colonel Duncan Eykyn of the Royal Scots
Courtesy: 58 Gorkha Training Centre

**Two Indian Field Marshals raise a toast**
Courtesy: 58 Gorkha Training Centre

army establishments and units where his wisdom and experience continued to captivate and inspire generations of officers.

All of this kept Sam on the go for two decades, but gradually the spectre of old age began creeping up on him. He was able to hold it at bay as long as Silloo was by his side, but with her passing in February 2001 the spark went out of his life. Brushing off family concerns about his health, he stoically held on to some of his directorships, dutifully attending board meetings, accompanied by Shul Bahadur. Shule would drive him to Coimbatore, sit next to him on the aircraft and stay in the adjacent room at the hotel; he needed an extra pair of hands to help him get by. At the airport he would often be accosted by obliging airline staff to jump the queue, but in spite of his frail health he would refuse preferential treatment and stoically stand in line and wait his turn.

In 2004 Sam was admitted to the R&R Centre[9] in Delhi with pneumonia. After a week his condition stabilised and he was discharged. The CO of the hospital and the attendant specialists lined up to see him off. 'Sir, you are as fit as a fiddle now, in better health than most of us,' they said, cheering him on. Sam thanked them politely, but as the car sped off, he turned to Maja and joked, 'Should I fix them—*hamna dhapi jaoon?*' (Should I kick the bucket right now?) But this time masked behind the humour lay the bitter truth; he knew his health was failing. ◆

---

9 Research and Referral (medical) Centre (of the Indian Army).

Maja with her parents
Courtesy: 58 Gorkha Training Centre

FACING PAGE:
Visting a solder's wife
in hospital
Courtesy: The Manekshaw family

# The Woman Behind the Successful Man

In 1937 Silloo Bode went to Lahore to visit her sister Tehmi and brother-in-law, Col. Kaikhushru Bharucha, a doctor in the British Indian Army. At a dinner party she was introduced to a flamboyant young captain who swept her off her feet. Two years later Sam and Silloo were married on April 22, 1939.

Silloo became the quintessential army wife, stepping up to wear the boots and keeping the home fires burning while her husband was away on assignment, which was more often than not in the early years of their marriage. Till 1946 Sam was either busy keeping the tribals at bay in the NWFP or fighting the Japanese in the jungles of Burma, so for the first few years of their married life Silloo stayed in Amritsar with her in-laws and saw Sam only when he came home on a spot of leave. In 1940 the young couple was blessed with a baby girl who they named Sherry.

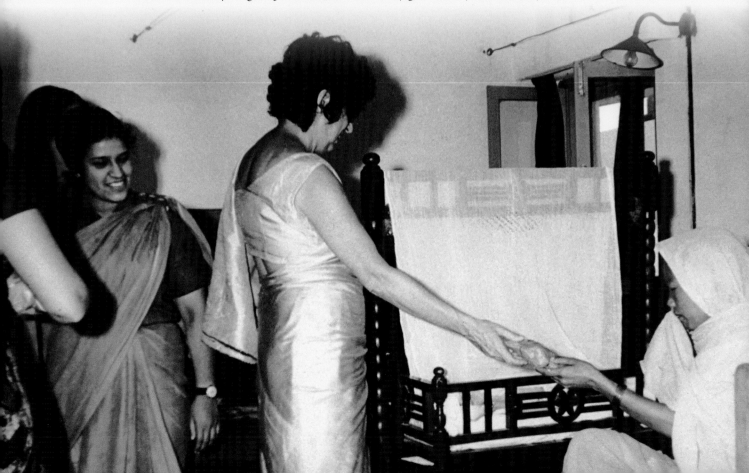

TOP:
The charming Silloo Bode

FACING PAGE CLOCKWISE:
The newly weds

The young mother with her
firstborn

The proud parents
Courtesy: The Manekshaw family

Silloo was an alumnus of Elphinstone College and J.J. School of Art in Bombay.[1] Painting was a hobby that she pursued with passion. A voracious reader, she was well informed on many subjects. She seldom skipped her morning yoga and evening walks and she loved a game of cards or mah-jong with the ladies in the station. Silloo melded easily into the army's social fabric and took great interest in all events organised in the station. She kept a beautiful home and made a gracious hostess.

To match her husband's altruism, Silloo's primary concern was for soldiers' families. She spent a great deal of her time and energy at the Welfare Centre[2] and made it a point to visit soldiers' wives or children who were admitted in the hospital to ensure that they received proper care and attention.

Silloo had her feet firmly planted on the ground. While her daughters, Sherry and Maja, were showered with love and affection, they were raised with a liberal dose of simplicity, discipline and traditional values.

When Sam rose to higher ranks Silloo was non-demanding of attention or special privileges. Never one for petty gossip or politics, even during the unsettling time of the infamous court of inquiry, she continued with life as if nothing were amiss. In fact she directed three plays at the Staff College, one of which was 'The Man Who Came to Dinner'. A member of the cast was none other than Lt Col. (later Lt Gen.) Inder Gill who was a DS at the college.

When I joined Sam in Calcutta as his aide, Silloo went to great lengths to make me comfortable and treated me like a member of the family. One of my fondest memories is of a trip we made to Bombay to bring back a new Fiat allotted to Sherry and Dinky. The road journey took four days. Silloo loved to drive so I was the designated navigator. We would get off to an early start and call it quits by sunset, spending the night either at a PWD[3] guesthouse or at a MES Inspection Bungalow. After a hot bath we would meet again for drinks, dinner and rummy. Silloo was the expert, I was the rookie, but during that trip I won every single game. If she found that rather strange, she made no comment. After reaching Calcutta, my overwhelming guilt caused me to confess that I had deployed every trick in my repertoire to win each game! It was probably

1 Sir Jamsetjee Jeejebhoy School of Art, Bombay.
2 The Welfare Centre in each unit looks after the welfare of soldiers' families, running adult literacy classes for the women and teaching them home-making skills. They also provide basic healthcare and immunisation programmes for the families. The CO's wife assisted by all the officers' wives presides over its functioning.
3 Public Works Department.

*Like a good army wife, Silloo distanced herself from official matters and never attempted to influence her husband's decisions ...*

her laid-back, casual attitude that emboldened a young captain to take such liberties with an army commander's wife. My successive wins had raised some doubts but my confession amused her as she dismissed my boyish prank!

As Sam often said, Silloo was both his most ardent supporter and his harshest critic. When he was nearing the end of his appointment as the eastern army commander, speculation was rife that he was tipped to be the next chief. The day of superannuation approached, but no announcement of his promotion was forthcoming. Just when he had resigned himself to his fate, Gen. Kumaramangalam, the army chief, called to give the good news that the government had approved his appointment as the chief of the army staff. He bounded into Silloo's bedroom and said, 'Darling, get up. I've just been told that I am going to be the next chief. Aren't you happy?' Silloo rolled over and said, 'I always knew you were going to be chief.' 'That's more than I knew,' he replied and went back quietly to his room.

Soon after their arrival in Delhi when Sam took over as COAS, Silloo came down with the flu. She drove to the Armed Forces Clinic on Dalhousie Road, half a mile from Army House, in her Sunbeam Rapier and stood in the queue to collect a token. When she approached the counter, the nursing orderly asked her the three standard questions: husband's name, rank and IC number. When he heard 'Gen. Manekshaw', he replied, *'Voh to Chief hain.'* (He is the Chief.) *'Haan, aur mein uski bibi hoon.'* (Yes, and I'm his wife.) The solider jumped out of his skin and out of his chair and ran to fetch the commandant who came post-haste to the waiting room and told Silloo she need not have taken the trouble to come to the clinic. As the wife of the army chief

**With battalion officers' wives**
Courtesy: 2/8 Gorkha Rifles

**At a Welfare Centre in Jammu**
Courtesy: 2/8 Gorkha Rifles

she was entitled to a house call. Silloo had to calm the commandant; she liked to drive, she loved to walk and she never sought preferential treatment.

Like a good army wife, Silloo distanced herself from official matters and never attempted to influence her husband's decisions especially as he rose to senior ranks. Those who approached her regarding postings and promotions got nothing more than a sympathetic ear. At the height of the 1971 war a journalist who interviewed Silloo hoping for a scoop must have been sorely disappointed for what she got instead was a damp squib. Yes, she knew about the war through the newspapers. She noticed that Sam had been coming home very late at night. Sometimes he spent the entire night in the office. That too she knew only because the orderly told her in the morning!

But behind this veneer of indifference was a serious and sustained commitment to the wounded and to war widows. The commandant of the hospital had been instructed to inform her when a fresh batch of war casualties was expected to arrive. The No. 2 staff car had been placed at her disposal. Regardless of the time of day she would be at the hospital, accompanied by Mona Batra, secretary, AWWA,[4] wife of Gen. M.N. 'Bim' Batra, and a group of dedicated army wives.

---

4 Army Wives' Welfare Association.

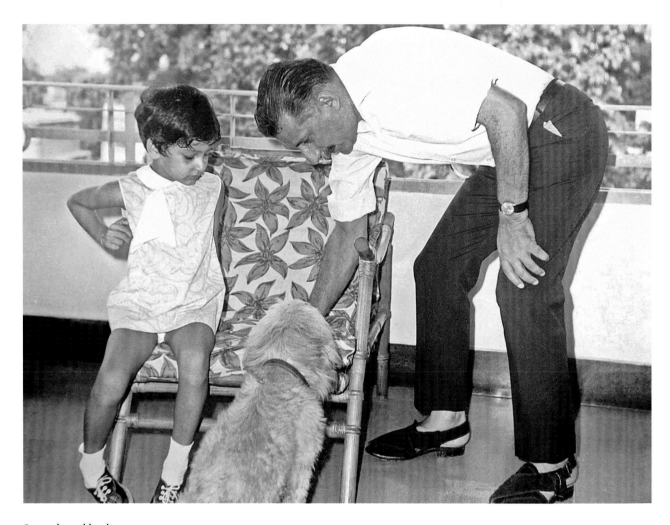

**Sam and granddaughter, Brandy, in Command House, Calcutta**
Courtesy: 58 Gorkha Training Centre

*... behind this veneer of indifference was a serious and sustained commitment to the wounded and to war widows*

Each day, along with AWWA members, she made her rounds, enquiring after the wounded, tracking progress, making sure their families were informed and helping convey messages and letters. AWWA members tried to bring some element of hope and comfort to soldiers who were incapacitated and to those with serious injuries, talking to them, distributing cigarettes and magazines and bringing a ray of hope to the despondent.

Pakistani POWs received equal face time, if not more. For the first few days, a young Pakistani officer at the Base Hospital in Delhi refused to acknowledge Silloo's presence. Each time she passed by his bed, he would turn his face to the wall and pretend to be asleep. One day curiosity got the better of him and he asked the nursing orderly who the lady in slacks was, who diligently came by each day and enquired after each patient. When he learnt that she was the wife of the army chief he was filled with remorse. The next day he awaited her arrival and apologised for his behaviour, saying he could never have imagined in his wildest dreams that the army chief's wife would go to this length. Silloo put him at ease and smoked a cigarette with him. He opened up to her regarding his hopes and aspirations to win the war and wept at the disappointment and shame of surrender. Her empathy was like a salve to his spirits. Thereafter, each day he waited impatiently for her visit and became her ardent fan.

# Brandy on her beloved Gramps

*My Sweet Gramps:*

*It is difficult to put into words the relationship I shared with my dear grandfather. He is known best for his great achievements in the Indian Army. For me it was far simpler than that, he has truly been the most noble soul I have been blessed to know.*

*My favourite memories are from my childhood, of quiet summer holidays spent at their home in Coonoor. Every morning he would take my hand in his as we walked through the sweet smelling rose garden which he attended to personally. He would teach me the names of flora and our conversations would be light hearted as he enquired about my life while providing unwavering and unconditional support and encouragement. I have often said, that although I doubt he knew it, he was the wind beneath my wings at a time I may have needed him most. His hands imparted every bit of what he stood for to me. They were warm, self-assured, methodical hands. Looking back, those times spent together were a foundation, for who I would want to become.*

*Sam had a rich sense of humor. His wit & imagination worked at lightning speed and we his family both benefited from and bore the brunt of his jokes. He was a great storyteller, regaling us with amusing anecdotes from his personal and professional experiences.*

*My grandparents were both giving people. Whether lending a ear or helping others to reach their full potential they liked to make a difference in the lives of others. I'd like to think that stemmed from being happily content themselves.*

TOP AND ABOVE:
**Sam being felicitated by film stars**

FACING PAGE:
**Silloo with grandson, Raoul-Sam, in Army House, Delhi**
Courtesy: 58 Gorkha Training Centre

Meanwhile AWWA's fundraising activities were her top priority. Silloo travelled across India to meet with heads of corporate houses, with members of the film industry and with donor agencies. She was able to raise Rs 2.5 crores[5] in cash and Rs 5 crores in kind. At her request Nasli Wadia, Chairman of Bombay Dyeing, donated blankets and linen to military hospitals that were facing severe shortages with the influx of patients. Sam used to say, 'My wife and I go around with a begging bowl so that my wounded soldiers and war widows won't ever have to beg.' When Sam and Silloo approached the private sector for the placement of disabled soldiers and war widows their requests were seldom turned down.

Silloo rejoiced in her husband's achievements in her own underplayed manner and when he was promoted to field marshal, she designed and gifted him a special ring with the crest of field marshal on it. Sam wore that ring throughout his life although he never wore his wedding band. But when the adulation for Sam reached a feverish pitch, Silloo ensured her husband was grounded in reality. As Sam put it, 'After the 1971 conflict with Pakistan and the swift victory which resulted, it became well neigh impossible for me to go anywhere without flatterers, fans, sycophants and hangers-on, comparing me to Rommel, Caesar, Napoleon and Montgomery. Just as I was beginning to believe it all, my Prime Minister promoted me to the rank of Field Marshal … but my down-to-earth, no-nonsense wife kept me in line, thus denying one more inmate to a psychiatric home, or what in India we would call a lunatic asylum.'

The citizens of Indore city honoured Sam at a public reception; Silloo was not able to accompany him on this occasion. On arrival he was heralded with cheers of 'Manekshaw ki jai!' (Cheers to Manekshaw!) The keynote speaker spoke in Hindi, heralding him as a brave soldier in league with eminent warriors like Rana Pratap Singh, the Rani of Jhansi and Shivaji.[6] Manekshaw responded in Hindi asking the organisers if he could have an English translation of the speech for his wife who spoke only a smattering and understood less. 'Every time I try to convince her I'm a big man, a great

---

5 1 crore equals 10 million.
6 Eminent Indian warriors who fought the Moghuls and the British.

**CLOCKWISE FROM LEFT:**
A family portrait in later years

Sam and Silloo on
their sixtieth wedding
anniversary

Sam and Silloo in the patio
at Stavka
Courtesy: The Manekshaw family

**Dr Renuka Devashayam
between Sam and Silloo**
Courtesy: Dr Renuka Devashayam

man, she ignores me. Perhaps after reading the translation she will believe me!' He brought the house down with thunderous applause.[7]

Although understated, Silloo thought the world of her husband. She was fiercely protective of him and did not hesitate to give short shrift to those who brought him grief. In 1969 we were attending an 'at home' at Rashtrapati Bhavan. Standing beside us was none other than Mr Krishna Menon who, in his heyday, had left no stone unturned to ruin Sam's career. Sam greeted him politely, but Silloo ignored him. Slightly embarrassed, Sam nudged her, 'Darling, you *do* remember Mr Menon?' Silloo stubbornly shrugged and said, 'Am I expected to?'

The clinic for the poor in Lower Coonoor
Courtesy: Authors

Non-demonstrative of affection, Silloo could come across as cold and indifferent to those who did not know her well. Under that veneer of indifference, lay a very supportive mother and an affectionate grandmother, a loyal friend and a caring 'first lady'. Silloo was often in the UK to lend a helping hand to Maja who was taking her Bar exam.

In later years Silloo devoted her time and energy to a medical clinic for the poor that had been set up in Coonoor, in a private home, in 1976, by Dr Phyllis Bellhart, an Anglo-Indian lady. The clinic was a volunteer organisation, run by the University Women's Association. Each time Sam went on tour Silloo handed him a list of medicines to bring back for the clinic, whether free or purchased. In 1994, when Silloo took over as the president of the organisation, she managed to persuade the Government of Tamil Nadu to allot land in Lower Coonoor. A small building was constructed and the clinic moved to its new home. Among those who rendered free services were several army wives. One of them was Dr Renuka Devashayam, wife of Maj. David Devashayam (2/8 GR), a student at the Staff College. Renuka recalls that while she wrote prescriptions Silloo had no qualms playing compounder and dispensing medicine.

The original objective of the clinic was to provide free check-ups, tests, medicines, and in some cases hospitalisation, mainly to women and children. This scope was later expanded to include a nutritional supplement programme for the young and the elderly. The clinic now serves 500 patients a month and has three regular staff, who are paid a monthly stipend. Patients are charged a token sum of Rs 3 per visit.

On February 13, 2001 after a brief illness, Silloo passed away in Coimbatore, leaving behind a very lonely and steadfastly devoted husband. Sam was never quite the same after her demise. ◆

---

7 Source: Obituary by Commodore C. Uday Bhaskar: 'A Legend in Uniform', *The Hindu*.

*In later years Silloo devoted her time and energy to a medical clinic for the poor that had been set up in Coonoor ...*

Sam with troops at 58
Gorkha Training Centre
Courtesy: 58 Gorkha Training Centre

FACING PAGE:
Sam's disarming charisma
Courtesy: The Manekshaw family

# I Did it My Way!

Over the years Sam Manekshaw had become a living legend, an officer with non-compromising morals who upheld the dignity of office. His sharp intellect, clarity of thought and decisiveness set him apart. So did his colourful speech which would oftentimes be peppered with hyperbole. His critics found this showmanship and flamboyance irksome. Sam was generous to a fault and forgave readily, including his detractors. Yes, he had favourites, but they were men of character and calibre, trusted lieutenants who worked hard and delivered. His shortcomings were few and far outweighed his sincerity of purpose and goodness of heart.

Sam's most outstanding attribute was his ability to reach out to subordinates. Maj. Gen. K.S. Bajwa (Artillery) recalls his first day as GSO1 at Headquarters Eastern Command in March 1967. The staff had gathered for the army commander's morning briefing. Sam entered the Ops Room and addressed Bajwa directly, 'Colonel, when did you come?' 'This morning, Sir.' 'Welcome! Did I teach you?' 'Yes, Sir.' 'Well then I can't find any fault with you.' Soon after Bajwa sent a paper for Sam's signature with a note saying, 'The army commander may sign if he approves.' Within minutes Sam was in his office holding the file at arm's length. 'Is this offending file yours? What do you mean by saying that the army commander may sign if he approves? What do you think I have brought you here for? If you consider that I must sign this paper, just say so and I will sign!' Six months later a brigade had to be urgently moved from its location to tackle an emergency. Only army commanders can authorise such moves, but since Sam, his chief of staff and BGS[1] were not in station, Bajwa took the initiative, moved the brigade and informed the army commander ex-post facto. Sam approved of his GSO1's initiative but pulled Bajwa's leg, 'Ah, now we are moving brigades without asking the army commander!' A few years later Bajwa was promoted to brigadier. He went to call on his old boss who had by then become army chief. Sam was presiding over the army commanders' conference, but within ten minutes he came out to congratulate his old staff officer. Bajwa rose to greet him but was pushed back in the chair, 'Ah,

---

1 Brigadier General Staff.

you have a lot of brass on your shoulders. Sit down.' Sam's parting advice was, '… remember, the higher you go, the more humble you must become.' This was his basic mantra.

Sam had internalised the motto etched on the walls of Chetwode Hall, at the Indian Military Academy.

He would instantly connect with the men he commanded. He made it a point to know his troops, the villages they hailed from, how much land they owned, whether they had availed of leave and how many children they had and if he thought that was one too many he would proffer free advice on family planning with a large dose of humour. The troops loved him and held him in high regard.

At *bara khanas* he made it a point to drink rum rather than Scotch, knowing full well that the subedar major and the troops would foot the bill. He would mingle with soldiers and their wives, joking and making small talk but wheedling out problems that are often kept veiled from senior officers and making sure they were resolved expeditiously. He would dance with the soldiers and add a liberal dose of *joie de vivre* to the evening.

As eastern army commander Sam was visiting a Garhwal battalion in Nagaland when a *safai karmachari*[2] stepped out of a basha and found himself face-to-face with the GOC-in-C. During visits by senior officers certain areas are 'sanitised' and all unnecessary movement by soldiers is prohibited. The nervous *karmachari* tried to beat a hasty retreat but Sam was quick on the draw. He grasped the man's soiled hand and placing an arm round his shoulder enquired after

**Chetwode Hall Motto**
Courtesy: 58 Gorkha Training Centre

_____
2 Janitor.

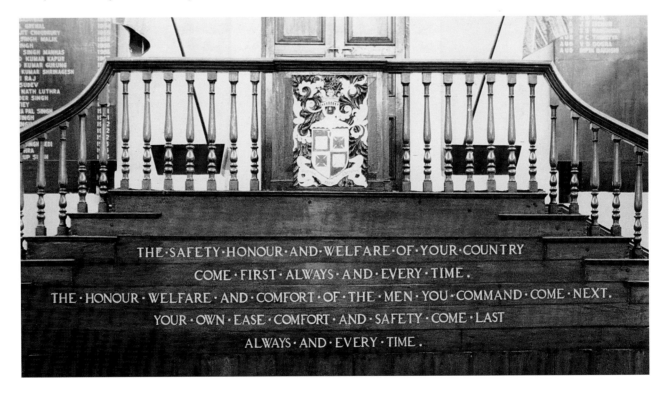

his well-being. While leaving he told the commanding officer not to punish the soldier for a minor lapse.

When Sam was chief, he was scheduled to go to Ambala. The weatherman forecast a cyclonic storm on the day of his visit and it was suggested that he cancel the tour. This to him was unacceptable, 'The Chief of Army Staff does not predicate his travels on the weather. What message will this convey to the men—that a little rain could scare away their chief?' Last minute cancellations smacked of indifference to the time and labour invested by soldiers to ensure that the spit and polish of the establishment was up to snuff.

Sam and Silloo went the extra mile to help those less fortunate than themselves. In 1947 when Sam was GSO1 in MO Directorate, Capt. Teja

A pat on the back for his stick orderlies
Courtesy: 58 Gorkha Training Centre

Singh Aulakh served under him. Teja had arrived from Pakistan as a refugee having lost all his possessions. He lived in Chattarpur on the outskirts of Delhi and cycled twenty kilometres to work each way. One dark, blistering winter evening Silloo was waiting outside South Block in the Austin to take Sam home when she saw Teja mounting his cycle for the long ride home. She offered him Sam's motorcycle that was collecting dust on their verandah. Teja gratefully accepted. A few months later Teja was nominated to attend Staff College in Wellington and on a Sunday morning he went to Sam's house to return the bike. Sam insisted he keep it, but Teja's pride would not allow him to accept such an expensive gift. In the end they compromised; Teja bought the bike for Rs 300.

Throughout his career Sam was very concerned that the army continued to be plagued with shortage of accommodation for officers and soldiers. Wherever possible he leveraged his influence to either initiate or expedite the construction of housing complexes. When 2/8 GR arrived in Delhi in 1970 it was garrisoned at the Red Fort. At a battalion function, a casual conversation with the wives revealed that many of the houses either had no geysers or geysers that malfunctioned. We returned home at 11.00 pm and despite the late hour I was told to call the GE at the Red Fort, 'Beroze, wake the bugger up if you must and tell him to report to my office at 9 o'clock tomorrow morning.' Within a week all officers' houses had functional geysers.

'The Chief of Army Staff does not predicate his travels on the weather. What message will this convey to the men—that a little rain could scare away their chief?'

Mrs Chopra, wife of Col. M.M.L. Chopra (Jammu & Kashmir Rifles), related an interesting encounter she had with Sam. She was living in SF[3] accommodation in Agra while her husband, a major at the time, was on field assignment. One afternoon she answered the doorbell to find the chief of army staff at her door. 'Sweetie, do I have your permission to look around your house?' he asked. Pleased as punch, she invited him in. The chief was dismayed. It was unconscionable that 'his wives' should live in houses that were poorly maintained while their husbands were deployed. The authorities must have received an earful, for within a fortnight all SF accommodation in Agra was shipshape. 'Sweetie, how long have you been living here?' he asked. Maj. Chopra had been on field assignment for five years. When Sam returned to Delhi he rang the MS and asked him to ensure that Maj. Chopra was posted to a peace station of his choice to make up for the oversight.

As chief, Sam fought many battles with the establishment to retain the special allowances and perks of army personnel. He successfully stymied a move by the Defence Ministry to reduce the two-month leave entitlement by putting forth a counter proposal to increase it because of long and frequent deployments. Narrating his own experience, he said, 'After my marriage, I went off to the war and didn't see my wife for three long years, except on short leave. When I came home at the end of my deployment, I found I had a brand new daughter and the only reason I was sure the child was mine is because she looked just like me.'

The Pay Commission tabled a proposal to discontinue Separation Allowance, a token sum paid to officers posted in non-family stations. In monetary terms the amount was barely adequate to

*As chief, Sam fought many battles with the establishment to retain the special allowances and perks of army personnel*

---

3 Separate Family accommodation is provided to families whose husbands are on field assignment.

LEFT TO RIGHT:
At a *bara khana* with the
boys

With the band
Courtesy: 2/8 Gorkha Rifles

Letting his hair down
Courtesy: 58 Gorkha Training Centre

keep body and soul together let alone run two establishments. Sam warned that a discontinuation would adversely affect the morale of the army. That too was stymied. This was followed by a proposal to withdraw the Kit Maintenance Allowance paid to all ranks to maintain their uniforms and accessories. Playing the consummate provocateur Sam invited members of the Pay Commission to his office and paraded in front of them, asking them to take note of his uniform, the perfect crease of his trousers, and the spit and polish of his belt and shoes. 'Now, do you think anyone will listen to me if I am dressed in a crumpled dhoti[4] and kurta[5] like a politician?' His caricature of the prototype politician had the Pay Commission members in splits and another essential allowance was retained.

Sam stood up to anyone who trampled on the dignity of his officers. When Defence Secretary Harish Sarin addressed a colonel as 'you there' and ordered him to open a window, Sam told him off. 'Mr Secretary, don't you ever address one of my officers in that tone of voice. You may politely request me to open the window, and I will. But no officer of mine is "you there".' Sarin backed off and said he had meant no offence, but Sam was adamant, insisting that he had not liked what he had heard, neither the tone nor the expression.

If Sam went to bat for his men, he was equally intolerant of those who circumvented rules. On taking over as chief he discovered that some officers had been gaming the system with mendacity to secure successive postings in Delhi on one pretext or other. The MS was asked to compile a list of the manipulators and every one of them was brought to heel. The few who tried to leverage political clout were threatened with dismissal.

---

4 Loincloth.
5 Tunic.

**A mug of beer at the JCOs'
Mess, 1/8 GR in 4 Infantry
Division**
Courtesy: 58 Gorkha Training Centre

When the occasion demanded, Sam could be curt and ruthless. As commandant, Staff College, he used to randomly review students' written submissions. A paper written by a rather supercilious student officer who had a tendency to hog the limelight was sent for his evaluation. Sam returned the paper with the comment, 'Seen and despised.' The young officer realised he had been sized up and reprimanded by his commandant and he promptly mended his ways.

Sam's reputation for unwavering rectitude preceded him. On completion of official tours bills had to be settled within twenty-four hours. Formations were informed that failure to present expenses would incur his wrath. Both his daughters got married after he became a general. He made sure the weddings were in Bombay, a great distance from his jurisdiction of command. They were small, family events with a handful of guests, no ostentation and no use of government resources. During his entire service, even when he was COAS, except for two orderlies and a guard that he was entitled to, he had no additional soldiers assigned to his house. For one month, when Silloo was in the UK and Swamy was on leave, arrangements for his meals were made with the Delhi Parsi Association.

The standard of integrity and probity Sam set for himself was the benchmark against which he judged his officers. When Sam was eastern army commander, his BGS went on promotion to command a division and returned to Calcutta a few years later as GOC, Bengal Area. Sam noticed that the officer was spending a great deal of resources renovating Flag Staff House. He also heard rumblings in the corridors of the GOC's indifference to the welfare of officers and troops under his command. After verifying the facts, on a Sunday morning the GOC was summoned to the army commander's office and handed his annual confidential report. The first two paragraphs extolled his professional competence, the third said it all, 'Now on the negative side, this officer, since his arrival in Calcutta, has devoted more time and effort to looking after himself and his personal interests at the cost of the welfare of his men …' Caught red-handed, the GOC was left with no option but to sign on the dotted line.

Sam's message was clear, he might grudgingly accept incompetence but he would never accept dishonesty. When he was chief, the case of a general who had indulged in financial misappropriation was brought to his attention. Sam called the general to his office and held his feet to the fire. Taking umbrage, the general retorted, 'Sir, do you know what you are saying? You are accusing a general of being dishonest.' Without pulling any punches Sam replied, 'Your Chief is not only accusing you of being dishonest but he is calling you a thief and a liar. If I were you I'd either shoot myself or resign.' The next day the general's resignation was on his table.

Sam was the first to let his hair down at social gatherings and encouraged his officers to follow suit so long as they maintained decorum. As army commander, he was invited to be the chief guest at the Raising Day celebrations of 5 Mountain Division in Tenga valley, NEFA. When the function got underway, an inebriate brigadier grabbed the mike from the Master of Ceremonies and began singing *'ragini'*, a traditional Haryanvi ballad. He urged the guests to join in and, when his request fell on deaf ears, he roughed up a young officer and upbraided him in boorish language, not realising that the microphones were on and everyone present was privy to the unpleasant exchange. Sam kept a stiff upper lip all evening but on his return to Calcutta he wrote to the brigadier, 'You are a bright officer with a good future in the army. If you control your drinking, your temper and your bellicosity, you might go far.'

Sam was uncompromising when it came to upholding the army's standards of discipline and performance. As chief, he was visiting the IMA at Dehradun and noticed that spit and polish of the barracks for gentlemen cadets was below par. He turned to me and said, 'Beroze, on our return to Delhi could you please send the commandant a crate of Brasso[6] and varnish. Obviously, they don't get any in Dehradun.' In the morning Sam took the salute at the IMA's 'Passing Out Parade' and the same afternoon he took the salute at a parade of Gorkha recruits who had completed their training at 58 GTC. Addressing the recruits he complimented them on their perfect turnout and excellent marching which, he said, was a notch above that of the cadets at the IMA! For the second time in the short span of a few hours, the commandant, IMA had been told off. But having

---

6 Brass polish.

Margin note:

*Sam's message was clear, he might grudgingly accept incompetence but he would never accept dishonesty*

conveyed his displeasure, Sam buried the hatchet. A few months later he was invited to visit Yugoslavia and the commandant was selected as his general-in-waiting on the trip.

Sam never held grudges, not even against those who had tried to diminish him. After he took over 4 Corps in 1962, Army Headquarters sought his advice on the promotion of two officers who had given evidence against him during the court of inquiry. Without animus he cleared both for the next rank. In passing he informed Lt Col. Vir Vohra, his GSO1 (Ops), about this decision. Vir, who had been a witness to the entire affair, was sceptical of Sam's decision and told him that both officers had shown lack of moral character, which was reason enough to debar them from higher ranks. Sam brushed the warning aside, 'Vir, don't nag me like Silloo.'

The principal prosecution witness during his court of inquiry was Col. H.S. 'Kim' Yadav of Grenadiers. When Sam was western army commander, Kim served under him as a brigade commander. Some officers tried to curry favour with Sam by running down Yadav in his presence. Bucking the trend, Sam said, 'Look chaps, professionally Kim is head and shoulders above most of you.' Word of this got to Yadav and over the years he was so overcome with regret that he felt compelled to mend fences. At the conclusion of the 1971 war he sent Sam a telegram which read, 'You have won the war all by yourself, without me. A remarkable achievement. My congratulations.'

Attending Staff College is an important milestone in an officer's career. Approximately 1,000 army officers take a competitive exam each year of which 300 are selected to attend the course. The first two on the merit list attend the Staff College in the UK, and the officer who stands third is sent to the Staff College in Australia. When Sam was chief, a major from Army Ordnance Corps[7] stood third on the merit list but the director, military training, recommended that an officer from a fighting arm should be sent to Australia. Sam overruled; if an officer had made the cut he deserved the reward, regardless of his arm or service. The ordnance officer went to Australia and rose to the rank of lieutenant general.

Soon after Sam became chief, the position of military secretary needed to be filled. He selected Maj. Gen. B.N. 'Jimmy' Sarkar (Armoured Corps) but Defence Minister Swaran Singh had his own candidate in mind. He turned down Sam's suggestion, asking him to cast the net wider and submit three names to the ministry. Sam was quick to smell a rat. He submitted the names of three outstanding major generals: Mahdi Hasnain from Infantry, Savak Antia from the Corps of Signals, and 'Jimmy' Sarkar from the Armoured Corps, thereby thwarting the parochial designs of the defence minister. The ministry acquiesced and 'Jimmy' was appointed MS.

When the Defence Ministry turned down the promotion of two competent generals Sam wrote to Prime Minister Indira Gandhi. Regarding the first, '… he is absolutely honest, and speaks his mind fearlessly. I admit he could be more tactful, but who am I to speak about tact? He is … dignified, straight, truthful and professionally good. I therefore feel that he should make the grade.' Defending the second, who had been blamed for failures during the operations of

---

7 The Ordnance Corps is responsible for procurement of weapons and equipment; it is not a fighting arm like Infantry, Armour or Artillery.

New family accommodation
in 5 Mountain Division,
Tenga valley, NEFA
Courtesy: 58 Gorkha Training Centre

1962 and 1971, he said, '… 1962 was a bad year for everyone, even if I had been in [his] place, I couldn't have produced better results. In 1971 [he] could have done better …. My only grouse against [him] was that he should have taken the blame for everything that happened in his Corps instead of blaming his divisional and brigade commanders. It is not a good trait in an officer to pass the responsibility for failure on to his subordinates, and hog the praise …. You must trust my judgement Prime Minister: … I am sure you will not take a decision contrary to my advice without first discussing the matter with me again. You and I hold views which are generally in conformity, it would be a great pity if on this subject we should find ourselves opposed. Naturally, I shall accept your decision loyally but I would again urge that you accept my recommendation.' In both instances he did manage to prevail.

Sam's biggest strength was his rapport with Mrs Gandhi. He had delivered on all counts and earned her confidence. She had given him free play in planning and executing the 1971 war, including the selection of D-Day which was to have been December 4, 0400 hours if Pakistan had not attacked us first. Four was his lucky number; he was born in April and married in April, his luck had turned when he commanded 4 Corps, and as chief his residence was 4 King George's

**Distributing goodies to soldiers' children**
Courtesy: 58 Gorkha Training Centre

Avenue. Was Sam superstitious? No he wasn't, but people in high places often have mendicants and soothsayers thrust upon them and his weakness lay in his inability to resist the temptation of playing along. When he was commandant, Infantry School, a palmist had told him that he had a narrow brush with death on February 22, 1942. 'I think you've got it wrong, I was wounded on February 21.' The palmist was adamant, 'Sir, you can cut off my head if I'm wrong,' he said. Sam says he told the damn chap he would, but as he walked into the house Silloo was coming down the stairs. 'Can you remember when I was wounded, darling?' 'It was the 22nd,' she replied. He could not help but notice another lucky '4'.

Sam's sense of fairness made him deliberate a great deal on cases of disciplinary action. Remembering the scraps he had got into in his youth, Sam was indulgent of junior officers. A young officer, smitten by a tribal girl, was indulging in an amorous dalliance with her, whilst unknown to him, outraged men from the girl's tribe had surrounded his hut and were baying for his life. Word of this standoff reached battalion headquarters and the commanding officer organised action to rescue the subaltern. Headquarters Eastern Command was alerted. The CO managed to retrieve the officer and diffuse the situation by reaching settlement with the elders of the tribe. A month later we were visiting the post. When Sam met the young lieutenant his only comment was, 'Boy, you had the whole of eastern army at "stand to", I hope she was worth it!'

As a young captain with 4/12 FFR, Sam had to deal with a similar incident in Burma. Two of his soldiers were caught in an 'Out of Bounds', red-light area[8] by the CMP and were marched up to him for disciplinary action. A court of inquiry established that one soldier was guilty of indulgence while the other had simply accompanied him for 'immoral' support. The guilty soldier was confined to the quarter guard[9] for forty-eight hours while the case against the other was dismissed. A few minutes later Sam had second thoughts. Soldiers spend a great deal of time away from their wives. Was the punishment too harsh? So off he went to the quarter guard and asked the soldier who'd been punished, *'Tumhara paisa vasool hua?'* (Did you get your money's

---

8 Visiting red-light districts is an offence in the army and such areas are declared 'out of bounds' for all service personnel.
9 A military lock-up where soldiers are confined for minor offences.

worth?) The soldier sheepishly replied, *'Nahi Sahib, kuch karne se phele hee CMP aa gaye.'* (No Sir, before I could do anything the CMP arrived.) Sam thought that was rather unfortunate and promptly reduced the punishment!

When Sam was eastern army commander, Brig. Rusi Cabraji, Commander 61 Mountain Brigade, complained that a major impediment to conducting successful counter-insurgency operations in the Mizo hills was the pathetic state of telecommunication infrastructure. No one could have assessed this better than Rusi since he belonged to the Corps of Signals. An indifferent Post and Telegraph (P&T) Department projected a four-five year timeframe to upgrade the network which was unacceptable to the army. Trying to work through a solution, Sam accosted a young SO[10] who was present at the briefing and asked how long it would take *him* to upgrade the lines. 'Two to three months at most, Sir, provided I have the stores.' 'And where are the stores?' 'At the P&T dump (depot) at Silchar, Sir.' 'So go get them, but don't get caught,' jested Sam. The SO took him literally and the next day he set off with a fleet of three-tonners[11] and brought back not just the stores but a wildly agitated and protesting P&T official in charge of the depot who objected to this 'pilferage'. This resulted in a spat between the army and the P&T and the episode was reported to Army Headquarters and received bad press. The army chief, Gen. Kumaramangalam, rang Sam for details and told him to sack the brigade commander and his SO. Sam assumed full responsibility for the fiasco. If anyone's head had to roll, it had to be his. The commander and the young SO got off lightly with charges of 'misdemeanour' but on the plus side within three months the communication infrastructure had been upgraded.

*What Sam valued most in an officer was courage. It was unacceptable for an officer to display fear in front of the men*

Sam, the young father with baby Sherry
Courtesy: The Manekshaw family

Sam's sense of fairness knew no boundaries. When asked if India's victory in 1971 could be attributed to the failure and incompetence of Pakistani military leadership, his response was honest. 'The Pakistan Army fought gallantly but they were outnumbered and outflanked. I had eight months for preparation while they were 1,000 miles from their base. We also had a numerical superiority of fifteen to one.' In fact, when Sam heard of the gallant attempt by Capt. Ahsan Malik of 31 Baloch Regiment to defend the Pakistani post of Hilli, he personally wrote a letter commending his courage and told Gen. Tikka Khan during both his visits to Lahore after the war, that the officer deserved a gallantry award.

What Sam valued most in an officer was courage. It was unacceptable for an officer to display fear in front of the men. He had learnt this lesson early in his career. During the Burma campaign

10 Signals Officer.
11 Trucks.

Sam was a major, commanding a company of 4/12 FFR. The battalion had taken heavy casualties and was facing a shortage of NCOs.[12] The CO held a promotion conference to review a shortlist of candidates. On that list was Surat Singh from Sam's company, a tough soldier but a badmash.[13] Sam did not support his candidature and Surat Singh was superseded. Word of this leaked to the unit lines and an infuriated Surat Singh threatened to kill the young major. During war, threats to kill are taken seriously and Surat Singh was disarmed and bound. When Sam returned to the company lines that afternoon he was greeted with an eerie silence, very unusual in a Sikh company. When he found out what had transpired, he ordered the company to 'fall in'. Surat Singh was marched up and charges read. Sam asked for Surat Singh's pistol, loaded it, handed it to him and told him to carry out his threat, whereupon the towering Sikh broke down, *'Nahin, Sahib, galtee ho gayaa.'* (No, Sir, I have made a mistake.) Sam admonished the soldier and dismissed the case. Later that evening Surat Singh's weapon was returned to him and he was appointed Sam's orderly. *'Surat Singh, aaj rat ko mere tambu par tu pehra dega, aur kal subah chhey baje mere liye aik mug chai aur aik mug shaving pani layega.'* (Surat Singh, tonight you will guard my tent and at 6.00 in the morning you will bring me a mug of tea and a mug of hot water for my shave.) The company subedar was alarmed at this turn of events and convinced that Surat Singh would kill the young major for the public humiliation he had suffered. Sam spent a restless night, alert to every sound and movement. At the crack of dawn Surat Singh entered the tent with a mug of tea for Sam and hot water for a shave and from that day on he became his ardent fan. This episode convinced Sam that all acts of indiscipline need to be nipped in the bud, and an officer must never cower in front of his men.

Sam's charisma was disarming; it did not take much persuasion on his part to make people do his bidding. We were headed to Dum Dum airport, Calcutta, to catch a flight to Delhi when the staff car came to a grinding halt. A young communist, perched on a stack of crates, was spewing Marxist doctrine while a volatile crowd had collected to listen to him, blocking the main artery to the airport. Before any of us could say 'Jack Robinson' Sam was out of the car and headed for the makeshift rostrum. The crowd parted while the speaker faltered and fell silent! Sam shook the man's hand and introduced himself as the eastern army commander who needed to get to Delhi for an important meeting. Now, would he be kind enough to clear the road so he could catch his flight? The budding communist was so awestruck that with a complete turnabout of purpose he began flaying his arms and yelling at the very crowd that he'd been inciting minutes ago to block roads, to disperse and make way for the army commander's car.

Sam believed that the *sine qua non* of leadership was decisiveness. His officers were advised not to procrastinate and over-analyse but to act expeditiously, except that he articulated this doctrine with his own brand of eloquence, 'If you must be a bloody fool, be one quickly!' He believed in action for '… an act of commission can be put right. An act of omission cannot.'[14] Sam decried 'yes men' as a noxious lot, used by superiors, distrusted by colleagues, and despised by subordinates.

---

12 Non-Commissioned Officers.

13 Bad hat.

14 From his lecture to the students at the DSSC, Wellington on 'Leadership and Discipline' on November 11, 1998.

*Sam decried 'yes men' as a noxious lot, used by superiors, distrusted by colleagues, and despised by subordinates*

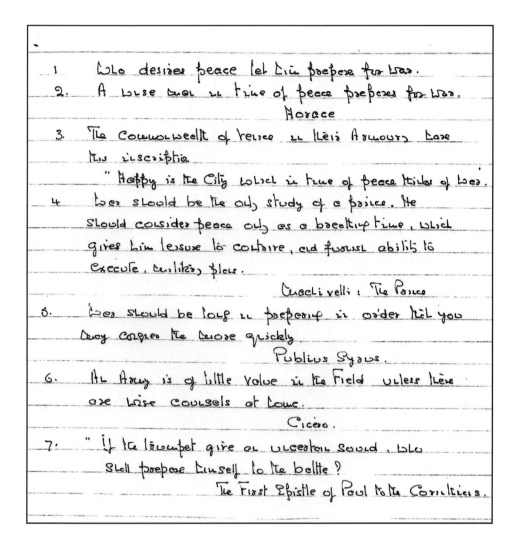

1. Who desires peace let him prepare for war.
2. A wise man in time of peace prepares for war.

   Horace

3. The Commonwealth of Venice in their Armoury bear this inscription

   " Happy is the City which in time of peace thinks of war.

4. War should be the only study of a prince. He should consider peace only as a breathing time, which gives him leisure to contrive, and furnish ability to execute, military plans.

   Machiavelli : The Prince

5. War should be long in preparing in order that you may conquer the more quickly.

   Publius Syrus.

6. An Army is of little value in the Field unless there are wise counsels at home.

   Cicero.

7. " If the trumpet give an uncertain sound, who shall prepare himself to the battle?

   The First Epistle of Paul to the Corinthians.

Sam's favourite quotes in his own handwriting
Courtesy: The Manekshaw family

*Sam's charisma was disarming; it did not take much persuasion on his part to make people do his bidding*

In keeping with these principles, Sam surrounded himself with men of character. One such stalwart was Maj. Gen. Inder Singh Gill. It was December 13, 1971 and we were in the thick of war. Things had not gone according to script on the western front; the Pakistanis had broken through our defences at Chhamb in J&K. There was pressure from the Soviet Union to move along expeditiously as it was becoming difficult for them to veto the calls for a ceasefire at the UN Security Council by Pakistan's allies, the US and China. Sam was tense and uneasy and summoned his vice chief, Lt Gen. 'Nata' Har Prashad and the officiating DMO, Maj. Gen. Inder Gill, to the Ops Room. Referring to the setbacks, he asked, 'Inder, what are we going to do about this situation?' Nothing could rattle Inder's cage. He grimaced, took his time, lit a cigar, inhaled, exhaled and drawled, 'I don't know what *you* are going to do, Chief, but *I* am going for a pee!' This was the perfect response to calm the COAS. 'Jolly good,' replied Sam, 'I was thinking of doing the same!'

Another officer Sam held in high regard was Lt Gen. 'Vir' Vohra. Vir was his BGS in Eastern Command. The army had plans to carry out the 'grouping of villages' in the Mizo hills. In order to deny insurgents access to villages and support from the local populace, it was decided to vacate

Talking points on Pakistan's military capabilities
Courtesy: The Manekshaw family

ADDRESS TO THE NATION DEFENCE COLLEGE
17 AUGUST 1979
FIELD MARSHAL SAM MANEKSHAW, MC

**PAKISTAN'S MILITARY CAPABILITY INCLUDING NUCLEAR POLICY**

1. INTRODUCTION.
2. PAKISTAN'S GEOGRAPHICAL SITUATION.
3. RELATIONS WITH ITS NEIGHBOURS:-
        AFGHANISTAN
        IRAN
        SOVIET UNION
        CHINA
        INDIA
4. PAKISTAN'S FRIENDS:-
        BANGLA DESH
        CHINA
        THE ARAB WORLD
        OTHER MUSLIM COUNTRIES
5. FROM WHOM CAN PAKISTAN GET MILITARY ASSISTANCE
6. PAKISTAN'S INTERNAL SITUATION:-
        NORTH WEST FRONTIER, INCLUDING DEMAND FOR PAKHTOONISTAN
        BALUCHISTAN
        THE POST BHUTTO ERA
7. PAKISTAN'S ECONOMIC SITUATION. THE INFRASTRUCTURE. INDUSTRIAL
8. CONSEQUENCES OF FAILURE IN WAR
9. WHY SHOULD PAKISTAN GO TO WAS AND WHAT CAN SHE ACHIEVE.
10. PAKISTAN'S ADVANTAGES OVER INDIA.
        A NATION ONLY OF MUSLIMS
        CAN EASILY BE ROUSED INTO HATRED
        HAS A BETTER SYSTEM OF DEFENCE CONTROL
11. PAKISTAN AND THE NUCLEAR BOMB.

*That a man so successful and so fair in his dealings had been so unfairly treated by the government was unacceptable to many*

them and move the villagers into camps, protected by the army. The army commander was under pressure to complete this 'grouping' before Christmas. Vir objected to the unrealistic deadline but was overruled. Annoyed with Sam, he stomped out of his office and told him to find himself another BGS. Two hours later Sam walked over to Vir's office, 'Sweetie, are you still angry with me?' he asked. He sat across the table from his BGS and together they drew up a more realistic timeframe. The operation was successfully executed. Sam could take as well as he could give.

Maj. Gen. Mohinder 'Bim' Batra (Corps of Signals, later Intelligence Corps) was a senior instructor at the National Defence College, Delhi during the 1971 war. Prior to this appointment,

Bim had been director, military intelligence for eleven years. On the third day of the war Bim was told to drop his teaching assignment and accompany the COAS to a meeting of the Chiefs of Staff Committee (COSC) of which Sam was the chairman and the naval and air chiefs were members. Seeing Sam's grim expression Bim asked no questions. Sam addressed the committee. The daily press briefings had been a disaster. 'Yesterday, a defence ministry official said our planes had bombed Murree (the hill station near Islamabad) instead of Murid (the airbase). For security reasons, he refused to give the name of the aircraft carrier from which our planes had bombed Chittagong. We have but one carrier in our fleet. Henceforth Bim will brief the press.' Bim was ill at ease with his new assignment but determined to be truthful, accurate and objective. He spent the next twenty-four hours preparing his brief. The next day, at the very first session, an overbearing American correspondent quizzed, 'What will you Indians do if the US sends its Seventh Fleet up the Bay of Bengal and lands its marines in the battle zone?' After a quick think Bim decided to quiz back—'Marilyn Monroe,' he replied. The journalist was confused and irritated and asked for an explanation. Bim replied nonchalantly, 'The marines I assume have been out at sea for a long period. They are probably so frustrated that they will first want to relieve themselves of the seven-year itch.' The press corps had a hearty laugh. Thereafter the briefings proceeded without a glitch.

Where was the army chief while the war was raging? Delhi was afloat with rumours that he had been seen at the 'Tabela', a popular discotheque at the Oberoi Hotel! It would not have been entirely out of character for him to put in an appearance for effect while leading the nation to victory.

That a man so successful and so fair in his dealings had been so unfairly treated by the government was unacceptable to many. Sam never dwelt on it, not even on the fact that his salary had never been revised. With a strange volte face in April 2007 the government decided to review the pay and perks of the field marshal and pay him arrears for the past thirty-four years that amounted to Rs 1.16 crores. They also offered him perquisites that had been denied at the time of his promotion. Defence Secretary Capt. Shekhar Dutt, SM (Artillery), presently governor of Chattisgarh, personally handed over the cheque to Sam at the Wellington military hospital. Sam scrutinised it with some measure of disbelief and asked if he owed the government tax on the amount. They laughed it off as a joke, but Sam had every reason for his misgivings. The perks included an office, two residential guards, two orderlies, a staff officer and a staff car. It was a case of too little too late that was offered only at the behest of President Abdul Kalam who had stirred the government's conscience. Sam turned down the offer of an office; at age ninety-three, when he was confined mostly to the hospital, he had no need for one. He turned down the guards as his life was under no threat and he needed no status symbol. He accepted the staff car and the staff officer to relieve the burden of care on his Gorkhas. His family was prohibited from using the car. When they came to take care of him, which was every few weeks, he insisted that his personal car be sent to receive them and see them off at Coimbatore airport. A week after his passing his daughters wrote to the government that car and staff officer may be withdrawn. The apple does not fall far from the tree. ◆

*Where was the army chief while the war was raging? Delhi was afloat with rumours that he had been seen at ... a popular discotheque at the Oberoi Hotel!*

'... I too would have come
with my war paint.' Sam
in conversation with a
Bollywood actress
Courtesy: 58 Gorkha Training Centre
FACING PAGE:
The tell-tale smirk
Courtesy: Authors

# Quirks and Humour

A smart military bearing with his handlebar moustache was the hallmark of Sam's personality. Often, Shubhi and I were asked if we had been ordered to trim our moustaches like his! To keep the mystery alive we hedged an answer and still do.

Sam loved to stand out from the pack. As commandant, Infantry School he wore shorts and Peshawari sandals to office during the summer. From the time he became army commander, like Field Marshal Montgomery, he took greater liberty with the dress code and jauntily wore a side-cap and a grey *mazri* shirt instead of the standard regulation beret and olive green shirt. I too had a preference for the *mazri* shirt and asked if I could wear one, especially since he expected his aides to dress like him! 'Beroze, wait till you have a few more pips on your shoulders!' was his smug rebuke.

Sam had some strong dislikes. He believed that only sissies carried umbrellas. 'What's a little water down the spine of a soldier?' He had an aversion for dark glasses after his commanding officer had snatched an expensive pair off his face and ground them underfoot, reprimanding him for ruining his eyesight. He never wore a pair thereafter, not even as protection against snow blindness! And he hated mikes. He was visiting a battalion and was to address a *sainik sammelan*.[1] A mike had been placed on the rostrum. 'Take this bloody thing off, I want to speak to my boys,' he said. In 1977 when I was a student at the Staff College, my syndicate[2] had been tasked to prepare a presentation on the planning and execution of the 1971 war. Armed with a tape recorder, I went to Stavka to 'debrief' Sam. On seeing the device he sent me packing and told me to bring Zenobia instead. She jumped at the opportunity and without much ado, reproduced what he said with exactitude. Time had not diminished his dislike for the offending

---

1 Akin to a town hall meeting where all the officers and soldiers of a battalion or a formation gather to listen to the CO or to a visiting senior officer.
2 Team of student officers.

*After winning the war Sam joked, 'I waited twenty-four years for Yahya's cheque to arrive; it never did. Now he's paid with half his country!'*

gadget. Sam never ate in public if he was in uniform; not on flights, and not at official functions like the President's 'at home'. As aides we were expected to follow suit; not easy to abstain when you are young with a voracious appetite and a good spread in front of you.

As large-hearted as he was, Sam took great pleasure in hoarding preserves and tinned foods. His deep freeze was a treasure trove of exotic delicacies: Parsi pickles, Russian caviar, canned fish, partridge and more. No one was allowed to touch these items or throw them away, even if they were well past their expiry date. The prerogative rested with him alone. Even the Gorkhas would lament, *'Kunne ke rakhe cha freezer ma!'* (God alone knows what junk he keeps in the freezer!) Sam also had a well-stocked cellar. He loved his family dearly, but when they left he would complain, 'My damn sons-in-law come and clean out half my cellar!' It was the same with good friends and colleagues. He enjoyed their company and feted them and plied them with drinks, but after their departure he would fake annoyance, 'The blighter polished off a whole bottle of single malt.' These were mere histrionics for in actual fact Sam was generous to a fault.

When he was chief Sam was on an official tour of Jhansi. Explaining Silloo's absence to Brig. and Mrs Bajwa he joked, 'Today is Saturday and not an auspicious day for her to travel. She married me on a Saturday!' Silloo was often the butt of his humour. When asked about the 1971 war he is known to have said, 'I know nothing about fighting; the only serious fighting I've ever done is with my wife.'

Sam's disposition to make light of serious situations was compulsive. When his father got to know of his near-fatal injuries, the old man of medicine cautioned, 'Son, you have been shot in the liver; if you drink you'll be a dead man. You have been shot in the lungs; if you smoke you'll be a dead man. You have been shot in the spleen; if you eat unwisely you'll be a dead man.' Narrating this many years later Sam would add his own twist, 'I obeyed my father, and almost died.'

As a senior officer, Sam often used a subtle mix of gravity and humour to convey his displeasure. When he was eastern army commander he was visiting a Garhwal battalion in the

The COAS with his wife (left) and daughter (right) and his ADCs, Captain Shubhi Sood (extreme left) and Captain Behram Panthaki (extreme right)
Courtesy: Authors

LEFT TO RIGHT:
Laxman's cartoon of Sam
and a near look-alike
photograph of him
Courtesy: The Manekshaw family

Mizo hills. After asking the CO routine operational questions, he changed tack and asked how many STD[3] cases had been reported in the battalion. The CO mumbled a number that was on the high side. To Sam this was unacceptable, so he queried some more, 'And how do you deal with them?' 'Sir, we shave off their heads.' 'What? I did not know that in the Garhwal Regiment you did it with your heads!' With that he turned round and walked away, leaving a rather bewildered CO who did not know whether to take it as a rebuke or joke.

When he was eastern army commander, one Sunday morning he was on the phone with Gen. 'Jaggi' Aurora, GOC 33 Corps. Business over, he asked Jaggi how he planned to spend the rest of his day. Jaggi said he was off to play golf. So Sam asked how long it would take him to make a hole. 'Sir, can't say. It all depends on my luck.' 'Jaggi, I'm always lucky. I always make a hole in one,' was the prompt rejoinder.

As COAS Sam's interactions with the defence minister were frequent. Traditionally the Parsi name 'Sam' is pronounced like 'psalm' though today the Anglicised version is more commonly

3 Sexually Transmitted Diseases. STDs are closely monitored in the army.

*He never failed to acknowledge that luck had played a great part in his career, and ... he would follow that up with, 'And the harder I worked, the luckier I got'*

**Done my time, paid my dues. What's wrong with a little booze?**
Courtesy: Mario Miranda Museum

used. Defence Minister Jagjivan Ram always called him 'Shyam'[4] which made him wince, 'Beroze, the next time the Defence Minister calls, please tell him there is no bloody "Shyam" here!'

During our visit to the USSR in 1970, we landed at Moscow's Sheremetyevo International Airport and were driven to our hotel. The liaison officer, Lt Gen. Kupriano, escorted Sam and Silloo to their suite and after making them comfortable, was about to leave when Silloo turned to the LO and asked if she could be taken to her room. Gen. Kupriano was completely nonplussed by this request. Sam quickly salvaged the situation by taking the general aside and explaining that since he snored and his wife suffered from insomnia, they slept in separate rooms. Then he whispered in his ear, that of all the women he knew, she was the only one who complained about his snoring! The general laughed heartily, slapping Sam vigorously and repeatedly on his back.

In 1947 when he was posted in the MO Directorate as GSO1, Sam owned a red James motorcycle. His GSO2, Maj. Yahya Khan, coveted this bike and made several offers to purchase it but Sam persistently refused. After Independence and just before Yahya's imminent departure to Pakistan, Sam relented and sold him the bike for Rs 1,000. Yahya happily took the motorcycle, promising to send the money as soon as he had settled down in the new country. Years went by and the cheque never arrived. Sam wrote it off as a bad debt. Many years later, when India and Pakistan went to war in 1971, by a strange quirk of fate, Sam and Yahya had risen to become chiefs of their respective armies. After winning the war Sam joked, 'I waited twenty-four years for Yahya's cheque to arrive; it never did. Now he's paid with half his country!'

When we went to Lahore to resolve the Thako Chak issue, Gen. Tikka Khan was at the airport to receive us in uniform and dark glasses. We set off for Corps Headquarters in frosty silence. The tension in the car could be sliced with a knife till Sam released the pressure valve, 'Tikka, why are you wearing dark glasses? You don't smoke, you don't drink, you have nothing to hide. It is I who should be wearing them!'

In 1972 we were attending a function at the Nepalese embassy. Sam was still riding a high crest of popularity after the 1971 victory and a diplomat's wife doggedly trailed him all evening. Suddenly he spotted Zenobia and me and made a beeline for us, accompanied by his ardent fan. Turning to the lady, he said, 'I'm sure you'll enjoy my ADC's company; he can sometimes be as charming as I.' While Zenobia and the lady were talking, he took me aside, 'Beroze, hang on to this beauty for the rest of the evening for if she comes within a yard of me I'll make sure you are in the dog house tomorrow!'

In 1973 after becoming field marshal and relinquishing office, Sam was visiting the UK. At a dinner he had hosted for the British officers, one of his old commanding officers walked up to him and asked if he could address him as 'Sam' now that he was a field marshal. 'Please do, Sir,' he replied, 'you used to only call me a "bloody fool" before. At one time I thought that was my Christian name.'

---

4 Shyam is the other name for the Hindu God, Krishna.

With the matron and
officers of Military Nursing
Service, while laying the
foundation stone of the
new Command Hospital
in Calcutta
Courtesy: 2/8 Gorkha Rifles

After relinquishing office Sam was on the board of fourteen companies including Escorts, an engineering conglomerate. The company had to change the entire board of directors to thwart a hostile takeover. Sam lost his directorship to a Mr Naik. In the Indian army a naik is equivalent in rank to a corporal. Sam commented, 'This is the first and only time that a naik has replaced a field marshal!'

Sam's humour was never sarcastic or malicious except when directed at the wily or deceptive. It is no small wonder that the witticisms that endeared him to men in uniform and the general public never sat well with politicians. He let the cat loose among pigeons when he rued the fact that our 'political masters who are responsible for the security and defence of this country cross their hearts and say they have never read a book on military history, on strategy, on weapons developments'. He questioned their ability to 'distinguish a mortar from a motor, a gun from a howitzer, a guerilla from a gorilla, though a vast majority of them resembled the latter'.[5]

Taking a shot at officers who had risen to the top by devious means, he expostulated, 'First, you should be willing to bend backwards to please every senior officer, even if the man is an incompetent fool. Second, you should have a wife who is willing to do anything to make sure you are ahead of the pack. Third, you should be a lucky soldier. Now, I leave it to you to guess how I rose to become Army Chief!' He never failed to acknowledge that luck had played a great part

---

5 The quotes are from Sam's lecture at the DSSC, Wellington on November 11, 1998.

The man who successfully walked the fine line between becoming a Field Marshal and being dismissed
Courtesy: The Manekshaw family

in his career, and just when you agreed with him he would follow that up with, 'And the harder I worked, the luckier I got.'

Sam never lost the common touch. One of his guiding principles was 'regardless of how high you rise, always remain a lad at heart'. He would lighten up a formal military function and put everyone at ease as soon as he entered the room. It was but natural that his best humour was reserved for his officers and their wives, his 'loyal troopers'. Sam joked with them, 'Thank God I am not a woman. I don't know how to say "no". Can you imagine? I would either have been permanently pregnant or permanently on the pill!'

Another strong lobby of support for him came from the Military Nursing Service (MNS). Sam would affectionately refer to the nursing officers as 'all my women', just as he would refer to army wives as 'all my wives'.

In 1977, when I was a student at the Staff College, we were at Stavka attending the annual 'at home' for Gorkha officers and their wives. Sam was talking to a group of ladies when one of them complimented him on his plum-coloured shirt. 'You see, love, all my clothes are from England. This shirt is from England, see the label on the collar, and this suit is from England, see the label here,' and then with a mischievous grin he added, 'so are a lot of my other garments, but I can't show you the labels here!' This was Sam at his best with his inner circle.

There were many exaggerated stories about his dalliance with the fair sex. If he got the slightest whiff of them, he would add more grist to the mill to create an even greater enigma around his image. Those of us who were close to him did nothing to dispel this mystery.

When Sam was in a pensive mood, he would reflect on the passage of time and the changing world with nostalgia, but shake it off a minute later with a dose of humour. In 1995 while delivering the first Field Marshal K.M. Cariappa Memorial Lecture in New Delhi, Sam talked of how the lexicon itself had changed since his days as a young officer. In the glorious 1940s the word 'gay' meant joyful, a 'queer' was an officer who enjoyed reading Milton indoors rather than enjoying sports outdoors, and only generals were entitled to have 'aides'.

Even with deteriorating health Sam did not lose his savvy mannerisms. In 2007 President Abdul Kalam was scheduled to visit him at the military hospital in Wellington. Just before his arrival a young woman reporter barged into his room, seeking permission to videotape the visit. Sam told her that he could not understand why a pretty young girl would waste her time recording the conversation of two old men but if she was prepared to wait till the president left he'd be happy to give her a private audience! With that, the young lady was tactfully ushered out of his room. ◆

*Sam never lost the common touch. One of his guiding principles was 'regardless of how high you rise, always remain a lad at heart'*

Nothing succeeds like
success
Courtesy: The Manekshaw family

**FACING PAGE:**
Sam's favourite picture of
himself
Courtesy: Authors

# Epilogue

After our marriage Zenobia and I moved into the ADC's cottage behind Army House. Shubhi had left for the UK. Sam and Silloo looked after us in more ways than can be enumerated. He'd be up at dawn, tending the garden with the *mali*, including ours. One Sunday morning around eight we heard a commotion. Sam had walked into our cottage and was asking the orderly where we were. I jumped out of bed, tidied up and was with him in a jiffy only to be reprimanded for being a 'lazy chap'. He said he'd be back in an hour and wanted a Parsi *'poro'* (omelette) for breakfast. Silloo was in London. Zenobia scurried to the kitchen, but that day the oil bubbled and frothed and every omelette fragmented into a zillion pieces. In desperation, she salvaged the larger ones and laid them out in a rice plate like pieces of a jigsaw puzzle. Sam arrived and tucked into the *'poros'*, passing no comment. She was relieved, thinking substance had trumped form. But how could Sam leave without a parting shot? *'Beroze, anneh paachi annhi maai na ghere mokul. Bilkool randhta nathi avartoo!* (Beroze, send her back to her mother's house, she doesn't know how to cook!) I can't afford to have an ADC who's not well-fed.'

Army House had a creeper overflowing with flat beans, *'papri'* in Gujarati. Two weeks later Sam asked Zenobia if she knew how to make *'papri maa kabob'*, another Parsi delicacy of flat beans and *kabobs*. Zenobia hadn't even heard of it, but this time, after consulting her mother, she was able to rustle up an authentic version and salvage her reputation.

As a married aide to army chief, the first challenge presented itself in the form of an official function at the DSOI. Mid-morning, Sam walked into my office, asked if Zenobia had been invited and what arrangements I had made for the evening. When I spelt out my plan to drop her at the club at 5.30 pm for a 7.30 pm function and to return home to escort him and Silloo, he cut me short, 'Boy, you must be crazy. She'll travel with us.' From thereon this became standard practice. In fact Sam went a step further; he made sure she was invited by personally letting the host know he had a married aide.

Sam to Zenobia: 'Are you
sure you want to marry this
man? You have five minutes
left to change your mind!'
Courtesy: Authors

*Sam continued
to be a frequent
and much-
sought-after
guest at
military colleges
and army
establishments*

Sam and Silloo had a long-standing invitation from the Birlas[1] to visit Pilani. After he relinquished office, the invitation was accepted and Sam informed the Birlas that there would be four of us. We flew from Delhi to Pilani and back in their private aircraft, visited the campus of the Birla Institute of Technology and Science, its enchanting museum, and the Birla schools, and returned to Delhi after a lavish lunch in their ancestral home, the Birla Haveli (mansion).

In 1977 I was nominated to attend the Staff College in Wellington. I had been allotted an army flat at Circle Quarters in Wellington, but on arrival I found the allotment had been changed to 'The Rosary', a private house in Coonoor. This was the furthest house from the Staff College. Annoyed and curious to know why the allotment had been changed, I went to the college the next day and was informed that the field marshal had requested the commandant, Maj. Gen. Adi Sethna, that his ADC be allotted the house closest to his. After that I had no complaints. In fact The Rosary turned out to be a dream home, a two-minute drive from Stavka. It was a sprawling bungalow atop a hill at the end of a long, winding driveway. In spite of sharing it with three other

1 A prominent business and industrial family of India that also runs educational institutions.

With officers and wives at 2/8 GR's 150th Raising Day celebration
Courtesy: Authors

student officers, we had seven large rooms, tiled floors, high ceilings and fireplaces, a large porch and a garden. During that year we spent a great many evenings with Sam and Silloo, catching up with news of old colleagues and reminiscing about the good old days in Calcutta and Delhi. It was almost like being aide once again, but this time with a family of four! Our neighbours were surprised to see Silloo drive up to The Rosary one morning to take Zenobia grocery shopping for she was convinced that my wife needed a lesson in bargaining!

Zenobia and I were well into the party circuit, often making it home only in the wee hours of the morning. Sam kept track of our social life, 'What are you chaps up to this weekend?', 'When did you return last night?' Soon after the course began, we decided to host an ice-breaker. I posted a notice on the bulletin board at the college, inviting officers and their wives who liked to dance to come to The Rosary with their 'bottle and dish'. Silloo was in the UK and when Sam got to know of this he asked why he had been excluded. Frankly, we hadn't thought he would be interested in a boisterous jamboree but were delighted when he said he would come with his bottle, his dish, and a friend. Sam arrived

**Old habits die hard …
Sam would always remain
in my charge**
Courtesy: Authors

with an attractive young lady. His dramatic entry was timed to get the rumour mills churning. That evening he was in his elements, mingling with student officers, dancing and generally sweeping the women off their feet with his charisma. Next day, predictably, the gossip mills at the college went into overdrive. The young lady he escorted had recently come by an inheritance and Sam was helping her put her house in order. She was so overwhelmed with legal and financial issues that he decided this was the perfect opportunity to introduce her to people closer to her age and give her an opportunity to unwind! A few years later, this young lady married an army officer posted at the Staff College. We left Wellington at the end of that year.

Sam continued to be a frequent and much-sought-after guest at military colleges and army establishments. Given my long association with him, if I happened to be posted in the town or establishment he was visiting, the army would appoint me his LO. When I was attending the Higher Command Course in Mhow in 1983, Sam came to address the students. In spite of his official commitments he had reserved an evening for us and another for all the Gorkha officers in station. In November 1984 when he came to Delhi for Indira Gandhi's funeral, I was posted at Army Headquarters and was assigned as his LO. In 1987, accompanied by Maja and Dhun, he visited me in Leh, when I was Colonel General Staff, 3 Infantry Division, and in 1990 he visited me in Delhi when I was commanding 35 Infantry Brigade. Often we would meet up with him at the Oberoi Hotel in Delhi and Bombay where he stayed when he came to attend board meetings.

In 1989 I was posted as an instructor at the Staff College in Wellington. By then Sam had given up some of his directorships to spend more time at home. I noticed that both he and Silloo were aging and had reduced their social engagements. I was in a state of enforced bachelorhood since Zenobia and the children had made Delhi their base. I visited Stavka frequently, and enjoyed the many evenings I spent with them.

In 1999 Sam and Silloo celebrated their diamond jubilee. At his daughters' insistence he gave Silloo a diamond ring, protesting, as he always loved to, that it cost him too much while the return on investment was negligible!

My next visit was under less than happy circumstances in 2001. We had moved to the US and I was in Bangalore on work. I had planned to drive to Coonoor and spend time with Silloo since I'd heard she was not in the best of health. A few days prior to my visit, she was admitted to

Visiting 3 Infantry Division in Leh (J&K)
Courtesy: Authors

a civil hospital in Coimbatore. I went instead to Coimbatore and spent a couple of days with her. From her hospital bed, she kept reminding Sam to take good care of me, especially my meals, little realising that time had moved on and I was now a very small eater. I was glad to have availed of this opportunity for it was the last time I met her. Silloo passed away on February 13, 2001 and was laid to rest in the Parsi cemetery in Ooty.

In 2004 Sam celebrated his ninetieth birthday. The army hosted him at the Battle Honours Mess in Delhi. At the party he joked that like everything else in his life he had entered the world the other way around. He was a 'breech baby'. It took his father forty minutes to straighten him and pull him out! He could still hold a captive audience in thrall.

But Sam was never the same after Silloo's passing. A bout of pneumonia in 2004 marked the beginning of the slide. He was in and out of the Wellington military hospital and in 2007 he decided to make the hospital his permanent residence. He could not be persuaded to live at Stavka and only went home when the family visited on special occasions.

Shul Bahadur stepped up to the challenge, spending the larger part of the day with him in the hospital to ensure everything was precisely as he liked it to be. He would cook his favourite

*He would not allow his personal comfort, even at the cost of his health, to override military protocol!*

With an old friend, Mrs Kalwant Singh, widow of Lieutenant General Kalwant Singh, his Corps Commander
Courtesy: The Manekshaw family

meal, minister to his every need and call Sherry or Maja with daily updates. Sherry made frequent visits to Coonoor to take care of him and the house. On one such visit she arrived at the hospital to find an overpowering smell of turpentine in the room. All the woodwork and furniture, including Sam's bed, had received a fresh coat of white paint in preparation for an inspection. Sherry felt stifled and was concerned for Sam with his fragile pulmonary condition. When she voiced her anxiety and threatened to call the commandant, he would have none of it. This was standard army practice prior to a VIP visit. He would not allow his personal comfort, even at the cost of his health, to override military protocol!

In December 2007 Zenobia and I were on our annual vacation in India and decided to visit Sam. Sherry came from Chennai and we spent five days at Stavka. Twice a day the three of us would visit Sam at the hospital. It was soon after the government had announced the payment of his salary arrears, and he had but one question for Sherry, 'Has my account been credited?' With a smirk he expressed serious concern that the cheque would be dishonoured!

In spite of his failing health Sam was alert. One evening we were running five minutes late. As we approached Wellington Gymkhana Sherry's phone rang. It was Shule, *'Time bhay sakyo, buro ley sodhecha ki kina puge chaina?'* (It's past time, the old man is enquiring why you haven't reached as yet?) We entered the room to find him lying in bed with his watch on his chest. During this visit we tried to jog Sam's memory, to make him recollect his days as a young officer. Most times he stubbornly refused to engage but when Zenobia mentioned the ongoing operations in Waziristan where tribal Pashtuns were giving the Pakistan Army a hard time, he perked up. 'That's nothing new,' he said, 'the tribals did that even when I was BM, Razmak Brigade in 1944. We would line our platoons along the highway at strategic points to protect military convoys.' We had found the chink in his armour. He carried on, recalling a brush with his brigade commander when he was BM. Each day he would prepare the SITREP and put it up for approval and onward transmission to Divisional HQ. But his brigade commander, whose name evaded him, was a procrastinator and the report never reached Divisional HQ on time. Annoyed, the divisional commander called the office one evening and asked to speak to the brigadier, who by then had left for the day. In the brigadier's absence Sam became the target of his wrath and was reprimanded for tardiness. He said nothing in his defence and patiently heard him out, but suggested he speak to his boss. That evening the brigadier invited Sam to his 'hut' for a drink. Appropriately turned out in a suit and tie he knocked on the door and was escorted by the orderly to the bathroom where he found his boss soaking in the tub and sipping a Scotch and soda. The orderly placed a chair for Sam in a corner and handed him

**Sam relaxing with his
newspaper at home**
Courtesy: The Manekshaw family

his drink. 'Look chap,' said the brigadier while scrubbing himself, 'because of you I received a rocket today from the GOC. He thinks you are the smartest bloody officer in his division with a good command of English and professional competence. Henceforth, I will approve all the SITREPs you put up to me without reviewing them. You know what that means, boy? You better make sure they are perfect.' 'Yes, Sir,' replied Sam, gulped his drink and left. There were no complaints from the GOC thereafter. This was the last story related to us by Sam. We had a strange premonition that we might not see him again.

A week before he died, complications began to set in. The family was by his side. The day before he passed away his daughters were in the room with him. A team of specialists, after examining him, walked towards the door where they stood in a conclave, conferring on his state of health. Desirous of being left alone with his family, he turned to Maja and asked, 'Have they left as yet?' When Maja replied in the negative, pat came his rejoinder, 'The blighters must be waiting for me to leave first!' He was joking about military protocol where the senior-most officer is expected to leave first. His sense of humour and his turn of phrase were as sharp as ever.

On June 28, 2008 Field Marshal Sam Manekshaw succumbed to pneumonia. He was ninety-four years young. His passing was a great loss to family, to friends, to those who served with him, to the army, and to the country. When we decided to write this book, many senior officers who had served under him, now in their golden years themselves, contacted us to recount their experiences with genuine affection. Some of them, not in the best of health, made the time and effort to type pages of their experiences! Such was the outpouring of affection for Sam that it humbled us.

Field Marshal Sam Manekshaw was born a Parsi and for the community he will always remain 'apro Sam' (our Sam). For the Gorkhas and for the Indian Army he was their very own Sam Bahadur. The Sikhs claim him as one of their own and the Tamilians are happy that he had made the Nilgiris his home. The Royal Scots will cherish his achievements while the burly Sikhs of 4/12 FFR will always remember their 'Jangi Lat' with pride as will the PIFFERs across the border in Pakistan. He belonged to all men and officers of the Indian Army, in fact to the armed forces. Above all, he belonged to all Indians. Even today he is a super-sized hero that each one of us can claim a bit of.

His passing marked the end of an epoch. He was accorded a state funeral with full military honours at the Wellington cantonment. The prime minister and the defence minister did not deem it necessary to attend. The vice chief of army staff attended as the army chief was in Moscow, but the naval and air chiefs deputed two-star generals who were on the staff of the DSSC to represent them. The national flag was not lowered to half-mast, the lame excuse being that the government had forgotten to add the rank of Field Marshal to the Warrant of Precedence. This indifference to a national hero is reflective of bureaucratic inertia and the depths of depravity to which we have fallen. The funeral of the Duke of Wellington, a British field marshal, was a grand affair in London, attended by heads of states and governments in Europe. In India, politicians who rush to attend funerals of business magnates and 'godmen' of dubious repute, displayed callous indifference to a soldier and a national hero. In retrospect, it was probably just as well that in death Sam was not subjected to the torturous lip service of those whose very antithesis he was. He was the people's soldier and in death as in life he was surrounded by people who loved and honoured him. Officers, soldiers, their families and civilians from all walks of life lined up at the Madras Regimental Centre in Wellington to pay their last respects as his body lay in state preceding a private, Parsi funeral. At a memorial service in Delhi, organised by the army, his grandson, Jehan-Sam, read the eulogy.

> *To Raoul, Brandy and me, he was always Sam, our most amazing, wonderful, and loving grandfather. He was the man whose thick finger you held on to as you were taken around the garden and made to memorise the names of flowers. The man who showed you how to wash behind your ears and tolerate extremely hot and extremely cold water baths without complaining. Sam took us everywhere with him and introduced us, emphasising the Sam, 'This is Jehan-Sam and that's Raoul-Sam.'*

*He belonged to all men and officers of the Indian Army, in fact to the armed forces. Above all, he belonged to all Indians*

Sam always wanted us to do things properly. His morning routine for example: waking up, putting on the BBC and setting his watch to exactly 5 1/2 hours ahead of GMT to the chime of the Big Ben, checking the mail in a particular order, going through the newspaper and folding it back for Silloo, showering and dressing in a particular order, until finally arriving at the breakfast table at 9 sharp. When we would stay with him during our summer holidays we would immediately be dragooned into doing this all with him.

Sam's capacity for fun was limitless. He would constantly joke with us, and gently bully us into getting ourselves into trouble with our grandmother. He would constantly check our grammar. 'Son, do I say I am coming to come?' 'No.' Sam, 'Then why are you saying I am going to go? It's wrong English!' He teased us until we learned to tease him back; he would play no end of practical jokes on us until we figured out how to avoid the booby traps and the ambushes. Finally, we discovered that we could speak up for ourselves, or even better, play the jokes back on him.

Sam at home briefly for his ninetieth birthday party
Courtesy: The Manekshaw family

Amul poster:
'Jai Jawan, Jai Sam!'[2]
Courtesy: AMUL and daCunha
Communications Pvt Ltd

*He brought lessons from his own childhood. The warmth of growing up in a loving family in Amritsar was something he so successfully passed on to his daughters; my aunt and my mother, and to his grandchildren. If there was one thing I remember that Sam wanted to share in a serious manner, it was the importance of family and loving everyone in your family.*

*People have from time to time characterised my grandfather as being too proud, or a little arrogant. But if he ever came across as being that, in actuality he was far from it. In his quieter moments, reminiscing about his life with the family, he would remind us of how lucky he was, and how blessed he had been to have life treat him so fortunately. He always knew he'd led an extraordinary life and he never took that fact for granted. 'I have always been a lucky man, and luck has had a lot to do with my success.'*

As Winston Churchill aptly said, 'We make a living by what we get, but we make a life by what we give.' Sam gave to India what has not been given in centuries—victory and honour. ◆

*Our God and soldiers we alike adore*
*Only at the brink of danger, not before;*
*After deliverance, both are alike requited—*
*Our God's forgotten and our soldiers slighted.*

FRANCIS QUARLES

---

2 AMUL billboards all over the country saluted Sam as a great soldier. AMUL is the acronym for Anand Milk Union Limited, a dairy cooperative in Gujarat state. AMUL's advertising agency, Messrs daCunha, is famous for its topical and cleverly crafted visuals and play of words.

# Acknowledgements

Our gratitude to Sherry Batliwala, Maja Daruwala, Freyan Panthaki, Jehan Panthaki, Sheroo Colabawalla, Rubina Patel, Feroza Fitch, Honey Mani, Fali S. Nariman, Former Additional Solicitor General-GOI, Lalit Mansingh, Former Foreign Secretary-GOI for their valuable inputs.

Sincere thanks to Lt Gen. A.M. Vohra, PVSM (Retd), Lt Gen. M.N. Batra, PVSM (Retd), Lt Gen. J.C. Pant, PVSM (Retd), Lt Gen. Vijay Oberoi, PVSM, AVSM, VSM (Retd), Maj. Gen. K.S. Bajwa (Retd), Lt Gen. Anoop Malhotra, Col. Vipin Patpatia, Sqn Ldr Rana Chinna (Retd) for their contributions.

Grateful thanks for their support to Maj. Gen. Ian Cardozo, AVSM, SM (Retd), Brig. Ashok Malhotra (Retd), Col. Pradeep Kala (Retd), Col. Naoroze Khambatta (Retd), Col. Manish Sareen (Retd), Col. M.M. Bhatt, VSM (Retd), Col. Chandra Shekhar Pant, VSM (Retd), Lt Col. A.K. Sharma (Retd), Cmde Aspi Marker, NM (Retd), Brig. Hemant Joneja, Colonel 8 GR, Brig. Manohar Thomas, Col. Vikram Heble, Col. Babu Francis, Col. Sanjay Kannoth, Lt Col. Amod Chandna, Lt Col. Manoj Handa, Lt Col. Neeraj Srivastava, Anita Anklesaria, Randeep Singh Arora, President Rotary Club, Amritsar South, P.R.S. Oberoi, Executive Chairman, The Oberoi Group, Dinshaw Mehta, President, The Bombay Parsi Panchayat, Cawas S. Panthaki, Excutive Officer, The Bombay Parsi Panchayat. ◆

# Index